SINGLE AND NOT SETTLING!

To Alison,

Thank you for all your support! It is a pleasure working with you!

Your friend - Boss (401),

Toni DeCosimo

april 2017

SINGLE AND NOT SETTLING!

A Journey of Surviving the Dating World

Tonia DeCosimo

ISBN: 0692832122
ISBN 13: 9780692832127
Library of Congress Control Number: 2017902725
Tonia DeCosimo, East Islip, NY

In Memoriam

Good fathers are a select few, a rare group embodying a confluence of rock-solid values executed with gentle hands and loving hearts. My dad was such a man—a tough, quiet, steady guy who made sure he was home every night to have dinner with his wife and children. This was a time for everyone to share what happened during the day and connect. Dad had a strong faith in God, and he believed in marriage, family, and commitment. He set a high standard for all men out there to follow.

My father faced life with a predictable ease and followed that formula to the end. I expected to complete this book a few years ago, but because of my dad's devastating diagnosis of terminal cancer, I put everything aside. Unfortunately, he passed after battling this disease for almost two years.

I dedicate this book to Michael J. DeCosimo Jr. He was not only a wonderful father but also a man I truly admired; I'm so proud always to call him my dad.

Contents

There is so much talk today about 'women power' and women making it on their own. Listen, I knew I could make it on my own; I didn't need a man to support me financially. But what about love? I realize that marriage may not be for everybody. I hear some women saying, "Who needs a man? I make my own money; I can go to a sperm bank." I get it. I had some of those same thoughts when I was frustrated with the whole dating scene. But I wanted love, a connection, a family. That's what I longed for, and I wasn't stopping until I found it.

Tonia DeCosimo

Introduction

A few years back, I started cleaning out a closet and found a bunch of love letters that had been sent to me over the course of my dating life. Some were loose, others were carefully wrapped with a pale-lavender velvet ribbon; they were all contained in a frayed box with that old-paper smell. Looking over those letters from guys who once meant so much to me, I couldn't help thinking about my life as a woman. I had just turned forty. I had a loving family, my own home, a successful business, and dozens of friends, but I was still single. I had no husband, no kids, and no prospect of having children in the near future. At that time I wasn't even in a serious relationship. I couldn't help wondering what was going on. I had no shortage of dates, but nobody seemed to be the right match. Was it the men I was meeting? Was it me? All I knew was that I didn't want to settle.

My situation was not unusual. The same thing was true for many of my friends. So many of us were still searching for love and not finding what we wanted. How did this happen? Why did this happen? Were we representative of statistical anomalies or statistical norms?

Gather a group of single woman together, ask why they are alone, and then sit back and listen to the stories they tell about how they have survived the dating world. Their experiences typically range from the dramatically sad to the hilariously funny in the "I laughed till I cried" category. Why do so many of us look at our lives and see histories that are littered with failed attempts to find and keep love? Why have so many of us met men who proclaim love in April only to turn on a dime and run for the hills in May? Why does the search for Mr. Right so often turn into a flight from Mr. Wrong? And let's not forget the ubiquitous question: Why have so many of us had so many weird or scary first dates? Does the process of dating and the search for love really have to be completely soul searing, heartbreaking, and traumatic?

Like many single women, I grew accustomed to having relatives and coworkers play armchair psychologists and try to find reasons for my single status. Some regularly accused me of being "too picky." My response: "Yeah, right. I turned down a wolf man. Something about the matted body hair and the dripping saliva dangling out of the corner of his mouth didn't mesh with my sense of style."

But if I were to try to give a more serious answer, I would have to say, yes, some women are too picky. I've known women who rejected men because they ordered the wrong wine or mispronounced a menu item. One of my friends wouldn't date any guy who wasn't a major stud; she insisted that each of the men in her life have buns harder than day-old Italian bread. I remember another woman telling me that she wouldn't go out to dinner with a man who had a funny-sounding last name. "Suppose he asked me to marry him," she said. "I couldn't go through life being called *Mrs. McGillicuddy*. And how about our poor children, having to spell it every day in school! How awful would that be?" But I honestly don't think that I personally was ever too picky. I just wanted to find someone to love for a lifetime and tried to approach the men I met with an open and accepting heart.

Several of the people I know told me that it wasn't that I was too "picky" but that I always made the wrong "pick." They looked at me and said, "You always choose the wrong men!" I always found this accusation particularly annoying. When you are a single woman, it's not as though you are regularly presented with a menu of possibilities. I don't ever remember seeing a line of single guys parading in front of me carrying signs that said, "Please Choose Me!" Single women are stuck with the choices that are available to them. Sometimes most of the pickings seem slim and problematic at best. Looking back over my dating history, I can't find any example of a time where I rejected a great guy in favor of one who was obviously less so.

Something else people often said to me over the course of my dating life: if you really wanted to be married, you would be. The implication was that I wasn't trying hard enough to find a husband. For the record, it wasn't about finding a husband; it was about finding the *right* husband.

Growing up as the youngest girl in an Italian American family on Long Island, I expected to be married young, teach school until my first child was born, and then be a stay-at-home mom. I envisioned a traditional marriage with kids fighting over the last meatball at Sunday dinner. That was my plan. I always had a plan for everything. But my life didn't turn out that way. Instead of being a stay-at-home mom, I worked on my career and built a business. Instead of having a husband, I had a long succession of dates with different men as well as a number of short and long-term relationships. I've had several proposals, engagements, and near engagements. I ended one engagement three weeks before the wedding. Everything had been picked out for the big day, up to and including the flavor of the butter cream icing for the cake.

I've tried to meet men in every way possible. I've met men through friends and work. I've made use of just about every modern technology available for Mr. and Ms. Lonelyhearts. I've done online dating as well as speed dating; I've belonged to clubs where singles are grouped together to meet other singles for dinner. I even went to a matchmaker. I've had short and long relationships with men who came with a dizzying array of contemporary problems.

I couldn't believe I was still single! Through it all, like most single women today, I continued to show up at my job every day; week in and week out, I did my work and tried my best to succeed.

I'm not a famous person; I don't have an advanced degree in psychology. I'm like a million other women. My book is not a solution, but rather an interpretation of life through the eyes of an average single woman. I like to think of it as a series of snapshots of the dating world as experienced by me and others I know. Throughout the book I have changed names and some of the details, because I'm sure the guy I met while speed dating, along with others, doesn't want to be easily identified. What happened during those five-minute "getting-to-know-you" dates in the lobby of the Hilton Hotel stays in the lobby of the Hilton Hotel.

1

Betrayal, Breakup, and Boundaries

It was a cold, dismal Saturday morning in early October, but who cared about the weather? I was in my little Plymouth hatchback driving to Ken's apartment because he and I were planning to spend the day shopping for *the* ring.

I wasn't exactly sure where we would be going, but on the north shore of Long Island where we lived, there were several obvious choices. We talked about going to Fortunoff's, well known for its high-end discount jewelry, but Ken's mother had told us about another store, and we also wanted to look there. If we didn't find anything we liked on the Island, we could always take the thirty-minute trip into Manhattan. Looking at my left hand on the wheel, I could almost see the sparkle that would soon be placed on my ring finger. My real life, the one I had been planning for as long as I could remember, was about to begin.

Here I was, twenty-three years old and feeling like the luckiest girl in the world, because Ken had proposed the night before. I had wanted to freeze frame the moment it happened. Both of us had been sitting on the light-blue sofa in my parents' living room, as we had done so many nights before. In front of us, the fire in the fireplace was doing its romantic crackling thing; to our left was the baby grand on which I remember practicing for so many years.

Without any warning, Ken turned to me and said, "Tonia, I love you. I want to spend the rest of my life with you. You love me, and it's time for us to get married. We can get a ring tomorrow."

Maybe it wasn't the most romantic proposal in the world, but it would do. I knew that he had already talked to my mother and father to tell them his plans and get permission. Ken was like a son to them; they were as thrilled as I was. We were all touched and impressed that he was following this kind of old-fashioned protocol. My life was proceeding as planned. Who could ask for anything more?

Ken, who had moved out of his parents' house when he graduated from college, was living in a studio apartment that was a short ten-minute drive from my house. Because I was so excited, I would be arriving at his place a little earlier than expected. This was 1992, too early for the average person to be carrying a cell phone, so I couldn't call to tell him that I was on my way. I had keys, and I figured I would just surprise him. There wasn't a bit of hesitation on my part; I knew he would be happy to see me. He always was.

Opening the door, I could hear water running in the bathroom. As I hung up my coat, I smiled to myself at the thought of my new fiancé getting ready for our big day. I knew Ken's apartment well. I had helped him move in; I bought the dishes for his kitchen; I was with him when he picked out his towels. This was very familiar territory. The door to the bathroom was slightly ajar, and as I moved closer, I could hear him laughing and talking. Almost immediately, I stopped smiling. It was his romantic voice! Let me repeat myself: he was using his romantic voice! He was practically cooing. I knew that voice well, but I had never heard him use it with anyone but me. The second I heard that voice coming from the direction of the bathroom, I realized he wasn't talking to his sister, parent, or friend. As I got even closer, I heard him say, "I have to take my mother out for lunch today for her birthday. You know how it is. But let's have dinner tonight. I'll call you. I should be back by five thirty."

What the…! It felt as though I had been kicked in the stomach. My response was immediate and powerful. Instinct and anger took over. When I walked into the bathroom, I could see him lounging in the tub, holding his bulky 1990s-style cordless phone with the antenna sticking out of the top. I grabbed it out of his hand. He stiffened, but he didn't say a word.

"Who is this?" I spit the words out into the phone. At the other end, there was only silence, but I knew somebody was still there, and I even thought I might know who it was.

Ken had been my fiancé for less than a day, but he had been my boyfriend since we were in junior high, more than nine years earlier. For nine years, he had been telling me how much he loved me. When we had been dating for a little over a year, he sent me a letter that began, "We have been going out for 375 days, 8,987 hours, 539,220 minutes and 32,353,200 seconds. Isn't that cool? I love you so much. I tell everybody that you are going to be my wife." Okay, so he was fifteen years old when he sent it, but still, it gives you some idea of the sort of thing I was accustomed to hearing him say to me.

Right now, however, he wasn't saying anything; his silence matched that of the person on the other end of the phone. He looked as though he had a golf ball stuck in his throat.

As upset as I was, I continued talking. "Do you know," I yelled into the receiver, "that this idiot asked me to marry him last night? Do you know that we are supposed to be on our way to pick out a ring? And now he's asking you to meet him for dinner later tonight?" I looked at my cheating fiancé, and our eyes locked together in a scary stare. "Well, why don't you meet him for lunch?" I asked. "Because I won't be going anywhere with him today! Or ever! You can have him! I don't want him!" I threw the phone down.

Okay, it was a little bit dramatic, but I didn't know what else I could do to express my anger and, yes, my pain. Then I walked out. I wanted to throw the phone in the tub, but I restrained myself from being that destructive. I don't remember him saying a word. And, yes, I forgot my coat.

From that moment on, I knew there was no going back. I didn't hesitate. I was completely out of there. I was also completely heartbroken. Ken wasn't just my boyfriend. He was my best friend! We had grown up together. But this time, he had gone too far. In my gut, there was a sick realization that if we got married, he would probably cheat on me for the rest of my life, and I knew I wouldn't be able to live with it. Ken was very good looking; I was accustomed to other girls looking at him. They would practically stop and drool.

But this wasn't about them—it was about him. And the question I kept asking myself: What kind of person proposes on Friday night and then makes dinner plans for Saturday with another girl? If we had picked out the ring as planned, why wouldn't he want to be out celebrating with me? I thought I knew him, but who was he? What was his story? What was mine? This was not supposed to be my life. Or was it?

How Did This Happen?

I honestly didn't know what I was going to do next. Alone and heartbroken wasn't part of anything I expected. Ken was such an integral part of my life that I had no experience in making the simplest plan without taking him into consideration. We had met in our early teens while roller-skating. In my home-town of Manhasset, Long Island, when you were fourteen years old and still in junior high, roller-skating was the kind of thing you did on cold Friday nights in January. I was with my best friend, Marianne, who already had a boyfriend named Victor. Ken was his friend.

Marianne was faster getting on the rink than I was; I was still sitting on a bench when her skates clunked to a stop in front of me. "Ken," she said, gesturing with her head in the direction of a good-looking boy, "said you're a fox."

He called me a fox! I didn't know exactly what that meant, but I knew that it sounded good. Ken was a few inches short of his eventual six foot two, but he was already exceptionally tall. And handsome! Did I say that already?

We began skating together awkwardly, in the way that young teenagers do. I stumbled and started to fall. I swear it wasn't planned. Ken grabbed me before I hit the ground. He was my fourteen-year-old hero! He took my hand, and we began to go around and around the rink together. The song being piped out of the rinky-dink sound system was "Let's Groove Tonight" by Earth, Wind & Fire.

Too soon it was 9:00 p.m. and time for my father to pick Marianne and me up. Ken and Victor's parents picked them up. We said good night, but not before we made plans to meet at the movies. *Porky's*, an R-rated movie, was going to be playing the following Saturday. All the underage kids would be sneaking in, and I could hardly wait to see Ken again.

When I think back to my teenage years, there is hardly a memory that doesn't include Ken. I grew up as the youngest child. Ken was the oldest of three children. We were typical teenagers of the times. Ken's bedroom was off the garage in his house. If his door was open and you peeked in when you were walking past—which of course I did—you could see the large poster of Farrah Fawcett in a wet red bathing suit. I told him that although my teeth were as white as hers, I didn't think I could compete in the bathing-suit department. He assured me that I could and that he thought that I was just as beautiful— maybe more so. How could I not love him?

We were both living on the north shore of Long Island. I went to Manhasset High, regularly ranked as one of the top one hundred high schools in the country; Ken went to a private Catholic school. I loved his parents, and both of our families attended mass at the same Catholic Church. He gave me my first kiss—a peck on the cheek in the back of the movie theater after watching *Porky's*. We went everywhere together. My family had a summerhouse in Bayville, which was further out on the island, and Ken would spend weekends there with us, sleeping on the couch. There was a rowboat near our house on the beach, turned upside down. We would regularly crawl under it to talk and kiss. Can either one of us ever forget the sand?

My father thought of Ken as a son. Much as she did for her own children, my mother knocked herself out preparing his favorite foods. She made him so much fettuccine carbonara that to this day I can't look at any kind of pasta in creamy sauce without seeing Ken sitting at our table filling his face. He definitely seemed like a full-fledged family member. He was my date for my junior and senior proms; I was his. Think four wrist corsages, four limos, and four hidden bottles of champagne.

The summer we were fifteen, we both got jobs at Lorraine Murphy's, a well-known local restaurant. He was a busboy, and I was the popover girl. That meant that I had to walk around with a basket of popovers, wearing a hat that I thought made me look like the Pillsbury Dough Boy. Ken laughed and told me I looked "cute." When I worked at the ice-cream parlor in Manhasset's large, expensive shopping center, known as the Miracle Mile, he would hang out to see me and wait for me to get off work.

I was a flag girl and captain of the basketball drill team and was expected to be at all the football and basketball games; he played lacrosse at his high school, so we went to each other's games. On Saturday nights we would curl up on the couch in my basement to watch *The Love Boat* on television and eat popcorn. Cuddling there, we shared all our worries, concerns, and family secrets.

When we were old enough to have driver's licenses, Ken got a motorcycle that his father didn't want him to have and my father didn't want me to ride on. But I loved holding onto Ken for dear life on the back of a Ninja, speeding down the Long Island Expressway on the way to Jones Beach. It was the best feeling in the world. I wasn't worried about getting killed on the bike; I was worried about my father killing me if he found out. Once, on a country road, Ken hit and killed a bunny rabbit. We both held onto each other and cried.

After high school, I went to Manhattan College, a Catholic school in Riverdale, New York. I wanted to be a teacher. Ken went to a college twenty minutes from me. We couldn't see each other quite as often, but we were still together once during the week and every weekend, and we talked on the dorm pay phone in the hall just about every day. It was a different time; we weren't texting and watching movies on our phones, we were doing real things. I remember beaches, picnics, vacations, long conversations, skiing at Hunter Mountain, and hanging out in the Jacuzzi with the snow falling around us.

I have to admit that it wasn't all perfect: we had our bad moments. And just about all these moments had to do with

Ken showing a little bit too much interest in other girls. There were a few times when I thought he might be cheating, because some girls I knew from high school actually told me, "We think Ken is cheating on you." Another time, he said he was studying with someone, but friends said, "Studying? That's what they call it now?" He denied it, but I knew in my gut it was probably true. We even broke up over it at least once. But he always said he loved only me and that he wanted to spend his life making me happy. I would remind myself how young he was and that he probably needed to sow at least a few wild oats.

That attitude all changed when he proposed. To be on the phone making a date less than twenty-four hours after we had agreed to get married! It was more than I could overlook or forget. There were limits to how much bad behavior I would accept to hold onto a relationship. One thing I was sure of: I didn't want to spend my life married to a cheating husband. This wasn't the life I wanted to lead.

However, I must admit that I often asked myself what would have happened if I hadn't arrived at Ken's apartment early. He and I ran into each other a few times throughout the years. During one of these brief exchanges, Ken said, "You know, Tonia, we were too young. If we had met in our twenties, we would have gotten married."

Tonia's Tips:
Learn from My Experience
Don't Allow Relationships to Be Wrong for Too Long

We say we are looking for committed, lasting partnerships. So why do so many of us waste so much precious time with people who will never be able to meet our needs? Giving people a second and sometimes a third chance when they hurt or disrespect me has been a recurring issue in my life, and I know I'm not alone in doing this.

My relationship with Ken is a good case in point. I should have split up with him the very first time I suspected that he was cheating. I know, I know: we were young, and it seemed like it didn't really count. But it did. If I had ended my relationship with Ken when I was still in college, when I was meeting, on an almost daily basis, what seemed to be an endless supply of nice guys, I might have had a better chance of finding my perfect match. But what was I doing during those carefree years, when I should have been dating up a storm? I was staying faithful and true to a guy who was out "studying" with someone else. Trust me, I turned down a lot of dates during those years.

The same kind of thinking applies no matter how old you are or what stage of life you're in. How often do we hear someone say "I should have ended that relationship years ago!"? Here's a question we can all ask: Why do so many of us stay in relationships even when we know intellectually that we are with the wrong person? Our hearts may be telling us, "This must be love," but our heads are definitely saying, "So why is he acting like such a jerk?" Why do we believe a miracle will take place and that Mr. Wrong will turn into Mr. Right? Are we just kidding ourselves, or is something much deeper going on?

Some women genuinely believe that they are so much in love that they will never be able to live without "him." They also worry that they will never again be able to love anybody else. If this sounds familiar, I would like to assure you: you will be able to live without this man who isn't treating you the way you deserve to be treated. You will also love again. That's because you are a loving woman. This is who you are; it has little or nothing to do with how he is.

I've interviewed multiple men and women on this subject. Most said that even when they knew there was very little potential for a healthy future, they continued to hang in there with the wrong person. Here are the most common reasons why we don't end questionable relationships.

- Fear of being alone
- Believing your partner is going to change, even though there is little evidence that this will happen
- Comfort with the status quo, no matter how uncomfortable it may be
- Fear of getting back into the dating world
- Ticking biological clock

- Trying to fulfill other people's expectations
- Worry that you're not going to find anybody better (when in fact, you could find somebody worse)
- Not wanting to admit that you have wasted so much time

Every single date and relationship we experience serves to define who we are and where we are going. Each romance, no matter how long or short, should help us refine our search for the right one. But how many of us wake up one morning with the realization that staying in our current relationship is like trying to fit a square peg into a round hole? We suddenly look back and realize we've spent the last five or ten months or even five or ten years living our lives clinging to false hope and a belief in change that will never come.

In my case and in life in general, I always try to give people the benefit of the doubt. I want to believe that if people make a mistake or realize their faults, they will indeed change. (This is especially true when that person is my romantic partner.)

One of the most obvious reasons why we stay with the wrong person is because we are afraid to be alone. Yet we all really know that being in a toxic relationship can make you feel even more alone, not to mention helpless.

We also stay in relationships too long because we are guilty of what many psychologists call "magical thinking." This is the belief that thinking or wishing something can actually make it happen. In the realm of love, magical thinking is driven by a yearning to want to find extra meaning and purpose in a relationship, even when it's not there. For example, we've all grown up with the fairy-tale idea of romance, and we look for our Prince Charming or Cinderella. Just like the storybook pair, we want to believe that we'll ultimately meet our lifetime partners for magical reasons tied to destiny or fate, not simply by coincidence. We convince ourselves we'll meet that person because we willed it somehow. Then when we enter into any new relationship, we experience wishful thinking. We want to believe that he or she is our soul mate forever, the only person in the world with whom we are meant to be. But if these supposed soul mates turn out not to be the people we originally thought they were, we desperately still want to believe in our dream, and we get stuck trying to make it work at all costs. So often, we exist as queens of denial.

Know What You Will and Will Not Tolerate, and Set Your Boundaries Accordingly

We each have a list of behaviors that we absolutely don't want to ever have to tolerate. I call these my non- negotiables.

Let's make a list of the most common.

- Lying
- Infidelity
- Emotional abuse
- Physical abuse

- Substance abuse (drinking and drugs)
- Financial instability and problems with debt
- Cheapness and lack of generosity
- Unkindness and dishonesty in his dealing with others
- Too much baggage (difficult families and exes)
- Extreme moodiness and negativity
- Bad temper and cruelty

You may have a few other behaviors that you don't want to ever have to accept in a romantic partner. It's important that you know yourself, so make your own list and put things down in the order of importance. Be realistic about your list. Remember, nobody is perfect, so don't be overly picky. But be clear in your own mind about what you will not tolerate. Know your own power: you chose to be in the relationship, and you can choose to end it!

2

Change of Plans—What Now?

Christmas. I'm looking out the window at the heavy snow; it's coming down almost as hard as my tears. Somebody in another room has on holiday music, which is making me unspeakably sad. But then everything is making me sad these days. It's my first Christmas without Ken, and my sense of loss is compounded because my parents sold the house in which I grew up, and we have made a permanent move to the beach house in Bayville.

In the blink of an eye, everything in my life had changed. I knew it was ridiculous, but at the time, I felt completely adrift and disconnected. I was positive that breaking up with Ken was the right thing to do, and I was more than a little proud that I had the strength to do it. When I walked out of his apartment, closing the door behind me, I learned something about myself. I learned that I did have limits, I did have boundaries, and my sense of self-respect was greater than my fear of being alone. This is important information for a woman to have about herself. But that didn't really ease my sense of confusion, heartbreak, disappointment, and, yes, anger. There were times at night when I was trying to fall asleep and I would unexpectedly sit up crying because I suddenly remembered what happened. I couldn't believe that "my Ken" had done this to me.

I wasn't the only one who was angry. My father, who had grown very close to Ken over the years, was furious. I felt guilty that my relationship had caused him pain. My mother, on the other hand, told me I should give Ken another chance. I certainly thought about it, but despite my overwhelming sense of hurt and loss, I couldn't do it. Maybe if he had gone on a thirty-day hunger strike and parked himself outside my front door with a large sign begging my forgiveness and proclaiming his devotion, I might have agreed with her. But that didn't happen. In fact, Ken's attempts to fix things were kind of weak. Yes, he came into where I worked to tell me that he loved me and we belonged together, but I knew that it wasn't enough.

But what should I do now? I was fortunate because I had a strong support system. My brother had moved out of the house into his own apartment, but my beautiful sister, Jolene, who was suffering from her own grief, was also living at home. Jolene's fiancé had been killed by a drunk driver the previous year, and she was understandably still working through her own unbearable feelings of loss. If my breakup with Ken did nothing else, it gave me an opportunity to get closer to my sister. We started to spend even more time hanging out together, which strengthened our relationship.

Also, my best friend, Marianne, and her high school boyfriend, Victor, had broken up six months earlier. For years it had been Marianne and Victor, Tonia and Ken. We did every-thing together. Now it was just Marianne and Tonia. I can't even begin to count the hours we spent on the phone reminisc-ing and propping each other up. Marianne, who was working in a video store, would bring home movies that made us cry into our popcorn.

As expected, we also tried to make ourselves feel better by trashing our exes. "He wasn't that good looking anyway," Marianne would say to me, as though either one of us really be-lieved that was going to make me feel better. I kept reassuring myself that it was good that Ken and I had broken up when we did and that it would have been much worse if I hadn't recognized his roaming eye until after we were married and had children.

How can I talk about this time of my life without men-tioning all the novenas that I did with my mother and sister? I may not have looked like one of those elderly Italian wom-en dressed all in black, clutching a set of crystal rosary beads, lighting candles, kneeling, and praying before a reproduction of the *Pieta* in any one of the Catholic churches in my neigh-borhood, but in my heart of hearts, despite my manicure and stilettos, I was still an Italian girl raised in a Roman Catholic family. on Long Island.

Like my mother and grandmother before her, when things went wrong, I was conditioned to immediately start doing a devotional practice known as a novena. That was part of my heritage. For those of you who didn't grow up in an Italian Catholic family, doing a novena means that you make a com-mitment to say a specific prayer for a measured number of days, usually nine. You often make novenas because you have a special request to make to a specific holy figure or saint. Some of my favorites included Padre Pio, who had yet to be consecrated, and St. Jude, the patron saint of lost causes. If my cause wasn't lost, I didn't know what was.

My very favorite saint, however, was St. Anthony, the patron saint of lost and stolen things. At that point in my life, it felt as though I was lost, and my boyfriend had been stolen. St. Anthony was definitely my guy. What did I pray for? I prayed that if it was meant to be—and if Ken had no interest in other women—then we would get back together. All the Catholic saints notwithstanding, I still didn't want a cheating husband.

When Ken and I broke up, it felt like a death, and I slowly but surely went through all the stages of grief, but not necessarily in the ordinary order. At first, I was angry and depressed, and then I started saying novenas to St. Jude (maybe that was the denial period). I prayed that if we were true soul mates, we would run into each other someplace and all negativity would be erased. We eventually did have a face-to-face encounter, but by that time I didn't want him back. I guess that was the acceptance phase. Through it all, I was glad that I had family, friends, and a job I had to get to every day.

Making a Living

Almost as soon as Ken and I split up, my friends started telling me I should go out and try to meet somebody new, but how could I do that? I couldn't eat; I couldn't sleep; I could barely stop crying. What I managed to do, however, was go to work.

Of course, there were those periodic trips to the ladies' room for crying breaks, but for the most part I held myself together.

I had hoped to have a teaching career, but the public schools weren't hiring. I did hear about one job at a Catholic school, but the pay was so low, I knew I wouldn't be able to make a living. Therefore, I was taking what I thought would be temporary work until I could find a teaching job.

From the time I was fifteen and old enough to get working papers, I had always had a job. I had jobs in restaurants, stores, and various local offices. I was accustomed to working, and I was accustomed to scouring the paper for ads and applying for anything that looked reasonable. Now that's what I was doing again.

My first job after college was as a part-time receptionist for a pharmaceutical company. They offered me a permanent sales job, but I was still intent on teaching, so I didn't take it. What I did take, however, was what I thought was going to be another temporary job doing phone sales for a company selling home security systems. I was working out of a typical sales boiler room with about fifteen other people, all of us sitting at desks lined up next to each other. Everything in the room was metal—desks, chairs, wastepaper baskets, office accessories—and there were no rugs or upholstered furniture to absorb sound, so it was incredibly noisy. We were a room full of noisy strangers, all on the phone, trying to make appointments for salesmen. It was probably the least glamorous job in the world, but I had been told that if I was good at it, I would get enough in salary and commissions to be able to make a decent living.

All of the salespeople in that boiler room were playing a numbers game. The more appointments we were able to make, the more money we would take home. There was little time for friendly chitchat. However, one day I must have looked more than a little upset, probably crying into my cardboard coffee cup, and the person at the next desk looked over and said something.

"What's wrong?" he asked.

"Oh, I broke up with my boyfriend," I replied.

"Oh, f——k him!" the person responded without missing a beat before he picked up the phone to make another call.

When he finished the call, he turned to me and repeated again. "Just f——k him! You hear me, darling!"

That was Steven. He was a tall, good-looking gay guy, about my age, but if he decided to arrange his face into one of several postures that he regularly affected, Steven was a dead ringer for Jack Nicholson in *The Shining*. When Steven looked up to say good morning, one could almost superimpose Nicholson's face peering through the hole he had just made with an axe in a splintered wooden door, and leaning in to say, "Wendy, I'm home."

Almost immediately, Steven, always funny, irreverent, and supportive, was my new best friend. He came home with me to eat my mother's cooking and help both of us organize our closets, an activity at which he excelled. In fact, one time he even tried on one of my mother's unflattering dresses and ripped the seams out Hulk-style saying, "Bea, now trash this!" Steven was even the driving force behind a large family estate sale.

At work, it turned out that I had an aptitude for sales. Steven and I were soon doing better than most of the others in the room, but both of us decided we wanted to make more money. Somebody told us about another company that was hiring. We applied, and after a half-day of training, we were selling another kind of product. Once again, it was phone sales. The company provided us with applications from people who had already shown an initial interest in being included in books of biographical profiles. Our job was to call, conduct the phone interview in order to gather background information about the person, and then offer our products and services.

What can I say about our employer, whose name was Syd? At one time or another, many men and women have put in their time working for somebody like him. Demanding as well as temperamental, Syd was successful, driven, brilliant, and a complete whacko. When he was in a good mood, he loved you; when his mood was afflicted, you could tell that he hated you… a lot. No matter what his mood, Syd had two primary sources of satisfaction: chocolate candy and a favorite brand of thin brown cigarettes.

Syd liked expensive things, and this was as true about candy as it was about furniture and cars. Although, when desperate, he might fall back on a supermarket chocolate bar or a Hershey's kiss or two, for the most part he was always surrounded by bags and boxes of high-end chocolate. The average family of four could probably easily buy food for the week on what he spent on expensive chocolate for the day. He was always either chewing on sugar or puffing on a cigarette, both activities that might help explain some of his mood swings. I quickly became accustomed to Syd's behavior, which included screaming, ranting, and the throwing of various objects against the wall. Syd's employees tolerated him because he was often as charming as he was temperamental, and he paid well.

I started out working in his Long Island office, where there were about eighty other salespeople working in two large spaces within the same office. The first space was for the people who had to prove themselves, but if you did well, you were moved up to a space that was referred to as the "black room." Everything in this room was black—desks, rugs, draperies. Everybody's goal was to make it into this space, because you got an extra hundred dollars a week, and everybody knew you were a top salesperson. Both Steven and I were soon working there.

It wasn't long before Steven and I were promoted again. Steven was made a manager, and theoretically I was moved to the decidedly upscale New York office, which was on Lexington Avenue, right across from Bloomingdales. In truth, however, Syd was never really sure where he wanted me to work, so I was moved back and forth from the Long Island to the Manhattan office, depending on where he felt he needed me most. I took that as a compliment. He also taught me more about marketing and soon had me writing sales material for the company.

My day often started at 5:00 a.m. so I could get ready and make the drive to Lake Success. On cold winter mornings, it would still be dark when several of us would be picked up in a parking lot and taken to Manhattan. Syd might then call to tell me that I needed to get back to the Long Island office pronto, so I would immediately have to cab it down to the Long Island Railroad at Penn Station and catch a train heading back out to the island. It was exhausting. My memory of that year is of crying in train stations and learning about sales. But I also met and established work relationships with people that would last for years. I learned some important things about myself during that time. I learned how to deal with pain and disappointment and how not to let what was going on in my personal life interfere with my ability to work.

One morning I woke up with a terrible sore throat and a deep cough. I called in sick and headed for my doctor's office. On my way there, on the Long Island Expressway, who should I see in the car next to me but Syd. He gestured to me to roll down my window, which I did.

"You're f——ing fired!" he screamed.

"I should be so lucky!" I yelled right back.

When I returned home from the doctor, I saw that Syd had left a message on my voice mail rehiring me and saying he wanted to promote me to general manager. So I went back for round two, asking myself whether I was making a mistake.

The time after my breakup with Ken was very much a learning experience. I discovered that I could and would survive the intense emotional pain associated with the loss of love. I discovered that I could and would be able to change direction, make new friends, find new goals, and discover a new way of being in the world. This was, as they say, a good thing.

Tonia's Tips:
Learn from My Experience
Transform Your Breakup into a Positive Learning Experience

When Ken and I broke up, I took a ride with a friend out to the Hamptons to relax and have lunch. When I broke up with the next man in my life, a friend and I went up to Hunter Mountain for a ski weekend. After my next breakup, my friend Susan and I took a trip to Paris and London. If nothing else, as time progressed I was able to afford better and more extravagant trips.

I think it's impossible to be part of the dating game for more than a few years without experiencing at least one traumatic breakup. Every woman who is trying to recover from the end of a relationship tends to think that her story is more painful than anybody else's. In the course of my dating life, I had more than a few breakups. For me, the first was probably the most difficult. After that, each of them was typically a little bit easier than the previous one.

I know that a broken heart involves actual physical pain. When a relationship first ends, it can feel as though the world is about to end. But it's not, it's just beginning. A positive transformation is taking place: a new you is being formed. You are evolving into a much wiser and more experienced person. Each of my breakups helped me become more in tune with who I was as a person and what I really wanted in a partner. I know the same will happen to you. Don't waste this amazing opportunity for personal growth by focusing on your pain and anger. Let the past go so you can move forward.

Remember: The Best Breakup Tips Have To Do with Attitude

Try to become more philosophical about your experience. If you broke up with him, I'm sure it was for a good reason. If he broke up with you, it's his loss. Either way, assure yourself that you will inevitably reach the point where you will be grateful that you weren't stuck with him for life. I realize that you may not feel this way at the time, but it is absolutely true. I have never met a woman who didn't come to this realization.

Don't Keep Second-Guessing What You Did or What You Should Have Done Differently

Of course some self-examination is necessary, but don't take it to the point where you beat up on yourself. If you insist on replaying various scenarios from your relationship, wondering whether your words or actions were contributory, you are going to waste a lot of time that could be better spent doing something constructive. If you can't get past the "he said, she said" thoughts, you're setting yourself up for a downward spiral.

Learn to Become More Forgiving

You need to forgive him for being such a jerk, and you need to forgive yourself for making the mistake of becoming so deeply attached to somebody who was so wrong. If you hold a grudge and you hold onto the past, you will never be able to move forward. Don't set yourself up for failure. Prepare and set yourself up for success. Try to look at your breakup in a more positive way. Take each relationship as a learning experience. Not everyone you meet is going to be right for you. People will disappoint you, and you will disappoint others. Just remember, each failed relationship brings you closer to a successful one.

This is your chance to embrace change and discover the art of self-reinvention. And don't ever think of yourself as a loser who failed at love. As the saying goes, you have to kiss a lot of frogs before you find your prince.

Try to Have Fun, No Matter How Rotten You Feel

Dozens of books and articles have been written about how to get over a breakup, and, at the risk of being repetitive, I'm going to echo some of the same advice.

Don't tell yourself that you're not going to feel better no matter what you do. It is okay to want to have some alone time and be introspective—but don't isolate yourself. Pamper yourself and do things you enjoy. Look for activities that may help lift those depressed feelings even for a few hours. For example:

- Take a trip with a friend (It doesn't have to be anything major. Even a day trip to a park or a beach can help improve your mood).

- Go shopping (my personal favorite). Just be careful not to use retail therapy to the point of maxing out your credit cards.
- Get a facial, a haircut, a manicure, a massage.
- Go swimming, take a walk, make a tennis date, or work in the garden. The endorphins from the exercise will lift your spirits as well as burn calories.

Keep reminding yourself: You are a terrific woman preparing yourself for the life and love you deserve!

3

Timing, Luck, and Questionable Decision Making

Recently, I went out to dinner with a group of women friends, and we began talking about the type of life decisions that might contribute to keeping a woman single. We all had histories that included at least one potentially good relationship that we didn't allow to move forward for reasons that seemed right at the time. We also remembered relationships, typically fueled by strong physical attraction, that we allowed to move forward even when we knew in our heart of hearts (also known as an intuitive gut reaction) that we were making a mistake. In retrospect, however, we wondered how our lives would have turned out if we had chosen or behaved differently.

When I question the wisdom of my own romantic decision making, the person who usually comes first to mind is Joey. In this case, there was nothing wrong with Joey, and I was the one who didn't let our relationship move forward. I met him more than a year and a half after Ken and I broke up. At first, I still didn't feel ready to be part of the dating scene. I had almost grown content in my safe little shell, telling myself that I didn't need to rock the boat by going out. I had also recently learned that Ken had married the girl from the tub and they had already had a baby, so I was a little upset.

But one of my cousins, who lived only a few blocks away, was having a New Year's Eve party. My mother and sister talked me into going, saying that if I was unhappy, I could just leave and walk home. Family is wonderful, but in my head, I could just imagine myself, probably the only woman at the party without a man, hiding out in my cousin's familiar kitchen, helping with the dishes. My uncle Jack would walk in, and he would say, as he always did, "Tonia, why are you here doing dishes? Why don't you get married already, so you can be home doing dishes for your husband?" Then he would laugh, and I would want to cry. My uncle Jack is actually a sophisticated guy, but something about the sight of me with my hands in soapy water scrubbing lasagna remains out of a Pyrex baking dish always inspired him to display his most retro Italian genes.

I went off to that party prepared to leave early so at midnight there would be no chance that I would be doing dishes alone and feeling sorry for myself. But it didn't work out that way: I met Joey almost as soon as I walked through the door. His first words to me were a compliment. "You look nice," he said with a smile.

In many ways, Joey was the ideal match for me. Like me, he was Italian and grew up on Long Island. He was smart, sensitive, kind, and sane. I loved his family; his family loved me.

There was nothing wrong with him! But there was one little problem. Almost as soon as we met, he told me that he had been working in London for a year. He was back in this country waiting to see if his visa would come through so he could go back to England. If it all turned out the way he hoped, that's where he wanted to be. However, I sort of got the impression that if he fell in love, he would be prepared to stay in New York State. Maybe he got the impression that if I fell in love, I would be prepared to move. Maybe we were both indulging in wishful thinking.

I do think we both fell in love, and we had a wonderful year together. Joey was a good person who was also easy and fun to be with. I always remember that when my dog died, my mother called him first. When I got home from work, Joey was there holding a dozen roses for me, prepared to help my mother break the sad news. That's the kind of guy he was.

As luck would have it, his visa was cleared, and the job in London called out to him. He asked me to go with him, but I couldn't do it. I was still young and wasn't comfortable about leaving my family. His attitude was that if I really loved him, I would move. Mine was that if he really loved me, he would stay. We briefly tried to sustain a long-distance romance, but we knew it wasn't going to work.

Did I make a huge mistake by not going with him? I guess I will never know. After Joey, I couldn't help but feel sorry for myself. Even though I had technically ended both relationships, it felt as though Ken left me for another woman and Joey left me for another country.

The next man in my life was another questionable decision. He was my boss. I had finally quit working for Syd and had taken a job with a similar company. My boss's name was David, and he asked me out almost as soon as I went to work for him. I told him that I wanted to help manage and grow his company, but that I didn't want a personal relationship. The company office was in Queens, he lived in Connecticut, and I lived on Long Island, so we started out with certain geographic and commuting challenges.

Our biggest issue, of course, was that he was my boss, which was why I was very reluctant to date him. This was one of those times when my gut was telling me to stay away, and ultimately I stopped listening to what my best adviser was saying. He kept asking me out; I kept saying no; he kept asking why; I kept repeating that I didn't want to date somebody I worked with, particularly if that somebody was my boss.

Eventually, he wore me down. One thing I will say about David: he was persistent, and he knew how to wage a campaign. He pursued and pursued. David, who was a very competitive guy, was accustomed to winning and getting his way. Here's a question I asked myself many times: if I hadn't said no so many times, would he still have been as interested? Was David just one of those guys who can't resist a challenge? Looking back, I think that was a distinct possibility.

David's campaign to get my attention made it easy to fall in love with him. To help you understand, let me describe our second date. David had heard about a restaurant/bar on the Island called the 56 Fighter Group. It was located in an airport for small planes.

"Why don't we go there for a drink?" he suggested on a beautiful evening in early spring. When we got there, David had another idea. "Why don't we go look at the planes?" he asked.

As we walked toward the dozen or so small planes outside of a hangar, one of the pilots approached us.

"I'll be your pilot for the evening," he said.

David had arranged for us to be flown to a lovely waterfront restaurant in Mystic, Connecticut. We had dinner there, and it was a magical evening. When David was good, he was very, very good. For one of my birthdays, he sent me twelve dozen roses. That's 144 roses! As I said, he really did know how to wage a campaign.

David was an amazing guy to date; he was so much fun. He was kind, courteous, generous, and we shared many of the same interests. David was also one of the few men I've ever known who enjoyed window-shopping and looking through upscale stores. He could spend the better part of an afternoon looking through Armani or Gucci with me. We wouldn't necessarily buy anything, just browse and look. Our tastes were similar, and we loved doing the same things. David got along well with my brother and sister, and my parents genuinely loved him.

So what was wrong with David? Some of my problems with David might never have surfaced if we didn't work together. When we were relating as a man and woman, it was good. When we were relating as coworkers or employer/employee, not so much. I was his manager, I was building his business, and I had strong opinions about how things should be handled. We often disagreed intensely about things that happened at work.

Let's be honest: there were times where I felt that David, who was a very macho, take-charge guy, couldn't handle having a girlfriend who had opinions about business as well as boutique shopping. When I went to work for David managing his company, he had five salespeople. When I left, he had about thirty. I wasn't just selling; I also did all the training and hiring. I was helping him build his business and making him a lot of money in the process, but I didn't have a part of it either in terms of final decision making or eventual profits.

My unhappiness with our work relationship convinced me that I needed to get another job. I wanted to separate the personal and the business. Once I stopped working for him, I hoped things would get better between us. In some ways, they did, but then other problems surfaced. After I was no longer in the office, I began to hear rumors that David was pursuing other women on the side. Was this true? Who knows, but the drumbeats were getting louder.

We had a few other significant problems. When David first introduced me to his mother, he didn't tell her I worked for him. In fact, he told her I was a teacher. It made no sense to me that he would do that, but he did. When his mother, a tall, beautiful woman with Nordic features who reminded me of Ingrid Bergman, found out the truth, she blamed me for the lie. I thought it made her dislike me.

This was a first for me; I was always everyone's favorite potential daughter-in-law. What I wanted her to know was how much I loved her son and how much I was trying to help his business succeed. Family is extremely important to me, and I was genuinely scared about how this was going to work out at all those future family events that would inevitably take place if we were together. How about grandchildren? What would happen?

My mother kept telling me to give it time. She was positive that once there were grandchildren, this would all sort itself out, but I wasn't so sure. I wanted a chance to show David's mom that I would be good to her, but she didn't seem to want to let that happen.

Other problems that kept surfacing had to do with David's moodiness. I sometimes wondered whether his moodiness was because he felt as though he was stuck in the middle between me and his mother. As our relationship continued over several years, I became more and more concerned about whether I could handle it long term.

David proposed several times, and—in what now was turning out to be typical Tonia fashion—I eventually said yes, and we decided to get engaged. A jeweler came to the house. I chose two possible rings. David was going to make the final choice and "surprise" me with a "nice" five-carat stone. We had planned to go away for an upcoming weekend, and I knew he was going to give me the ring to make our engagement official.

A week before this was supposed to take place, David and I had a date, but he didn't show up. I waited for hours and phoned him several times. No answer. He finally called and told me that he had been out on a boat with friends. Instead of apologizing for keeping me waiting, he got nasty, and I got upset.

This wasn't the first time this had happened. I realized that I loved him, but I didn't want to marry him. The intensity of the anger between us had become scary. The time had come to move on. We both slammed down our respective phones—and, as amazing as it may seem, given everything that had existed between us, we never spoke again.

I ran into him about a year or so later—appropriately enough, in the oceanside restaurant where we had been on our first date. I was sitting at a table, when I felt a familiar hand on my shoulder. It was David.

"Hi," he said, "how are you?"

I had really loved David, and meeting him like this was very emotional for me. Fortunately, I was wearing sunglasses, so he couldn't see my tears. When he left the table, I went into the ladies' room to try to calm down. I asked myself whether I should go over to his table and try to talk to him. I wondered if running into him like this was an opportunity and a message that I should try to get back with him. I was so flustered that when I saw a spray can near the sink, I grabbed it and sprayed my hair, assuming it was hairspray. It was Lysol. What more can I say? I wasn't going to approach any man smelling like lemon-scented antiseptic.

Attraction versus Intuition

With every failed relationship, we mourn a little and learn a lot. Sure, I could have married and been happy for a time, while I managed to overlook underlying problems, but eventually I would have probably been miserable and ultimately divorced. Wouldn't that have wasted even more precious time? With David, there was a deep love, but I still ask myself how I allowed things to go so far astray and for so long. I don't have all the answers, but I guess I couldn't ignore the love combined with the chemistry.

When my women friends and I talk about some of our failed relationships, inevitably we agree that when these relationships started, we knew intuitively that there were basic problems that we decided to overlook because of physical attraction.

The next logical question is, Why do we regularly allow physical attraction to override intuition? Have you ever noticed that if you walk into a party, bar, or any other room filled with potential mates, one will always grab your attention, while the others fade to a shadowy gray? The aura on the one you're attracted to glows brighter than it does on any of the others. Do you notice how you feel flustered, and your heart beats faster? Is that chemistry, physical attraction, or conditioning? In a series of nanosecond flash encounters, why does one person stand out over all the rest?

I never seemed to outgrow that burst of excitement that erupted when a potential romantic partner appeared. Suddenly, all the layers of cynicism would peel away and reveal another layer of hope, along with a willingness to plunge into a new relationship and start all over again. But I never understood it.

I would like to think that chemistry and physical attraction were not that important to me, but in reality I fell victim to the lure of good chemistry more than once. I'd meet someone and be drawn to him instantly without a thought as to why. The euphoria would then carry me blindly into the next phase. I would feel as though I was in love. But was I really only in lust? Down the road, as the relationship unfolded and reason returned, I would get angry at myself for not showing more wisdom in my initial choice. Whatever possessed me to follow this guy off the cliff? I would ask myself, Why didn't I see this coming? Clearly this relationship had "doomed" written all over it, but I followed him anyway. And, of course, I always paid the price.

When we are going through our own relationship problems, we tend to want to believe that our feelings of intense attraction are unique to our lives and our lives alone. But that's really not the case. It took under ten minutes of Googling to discover that scientists and biologists have been dissecting the subject of physical attraction and chemistry for decades. They go so far as to describe this phenomenon as a law of attraction that is written in our DNA. We come programmed with specific preferences passed down through generations of development and natural selection, so our choices are neither as random nor as simple as they first appear.

We have all experienced that indescribable feeling that occurs when we meet someone and all of our senses automatically kick in. Many of these responses are conscious, while others are set off in our subconscious. Appearance, scent, body shape, and a host of other triggers generate an automatic reaction. The fluttering heart and sweaty palms that routinely respond to the same irresistible type can be blamed on our DNA profile. So if your preferences defy logic, don't worry. I discovered that even members of the scientific community disagree with each other's research and findings. The debate of nature versus nurture is never-ending.

The type of person who makes us put reason aside can be traced back to our prehistoric ancestors, who sought partners primarily for purposes of breeding. Your brain and my brain are both hardwired to be attracted to people with even features and strong bodies because they illustrate health and vigor, qualities necessary for reproduction. Most men prefer a woman with curves, a tucked waist, and expressive eyes. Women swoon over hard bodies, broad shoulders, and a whiff of just the right scent of sweat. Sex was designed to ensure the continuation of life. We may have abandoned or overlooked its original intention, but desire cannot be denied. Ask any guy how many times a day sex enters his thoughts. Do we have a mainframe large enough for the calculation?

Reading about all this research left me quite dumbfounded. Of course, this research has some serious applications and deserves respect, but really, how much of this prehistoric hormone-twisting information directly applies to the average man and woman? I was interested in finding more defined relationship data that went beyond laboratory charts, experiments with mice that simultaneously emit different scents to both genders, and female monkeys whose butts flame as red as a traffic light when they are interested in procreation.

Advertisers realize that sex sells, and they have dissected the same studies that I found. Big business manufactures products that seize every opportunity to trick our senses and exploit our weaknesses. Pheromones, chemical signals produced by our bodies to communicate sexual reproductive qualities, have sparked the interest of perfume manufacturers worldwide. New fragrances come on the market daily from celebrities as well as clothing and cosmetic lines. Marketing plays a big role in our choices. Unlike elephants, which have kept their basic instincts intact, humankind has lost many of its instincts to evolution and modern technologies. It goes without saying that in the jungles of New York, Chicago, and Los Angeles, singles have different sexual triggers than monkeys and bull elephants have in their natural habitats. Pollution combined with the smell of hot asphalt has undoubtedly wreaked havoc on our human responses, disengaging the natural connection we once enjoyed in our pristine ancient habitat.

Experts might disagree about which law or rule of attraction rates number one, but when it comes to hormones and the human heart, not one brainiac has cracked the code. Evolution, society, family environments, and our genetic makeup all influence our choices. Singletons don't usually exist in the wild. There, every creature has a mate, although some of these partnerships might barely last for the afternoon.

If a modern woman's only task were to have children, she would simply go to the sperm bank and put in her order for offspring. Problem solved. She could skip steps one and two, and all the preening and perfuming would be superfluous. Bloomingdale's, Saks, and the cosmetic counters at the local malls might go under. But humans are at the top of the animal kingdom and have evolved into sophisticated creatures with complex needs. Along with basic instincts, we have something else that appears to be absent in animals. We have egos. Lord, help us!

I agree that physical attraction and good chemistry will jumpstart any relationship, but if a relationship is primarily flamed by sex, and it ignites too quickly, there is a good chance that it will die out with equal speed. Sex might masquerade as love, but great sex doesn't automatically translate into an enduring partnership. Let me see if I have this right: fabulous sex alone can't hold a couple together, but can a relationship survive without some sensational sex? Men and women who cheat sometimes claim that poor sex or lack of sex is the main reason for their infidelity—but are cheaters a reliable source of information?

In my own case, I don't have all the answers, but I do know that there were too many times when I allowed physical attraction to overrule initial intuition. However, the opposite is also the case: I once dated a man I liked who really wasn't my physical type. He was kind, sincere, and successful, and we had a lot in common. Despite his many fine attributes and his declaration that he would be devoted to the grave, once we'd swapped saliva, I knew that intimacy with him was inconceivable. All my senses triggered a response that screamed, "Get me out of here!" My reactions reminded me of what my father told my mother after she served him *capozzella* (a grilled sheep's head) for dinner. "You did it once; don't do it again."

Tonia's Tips:
Learn from My Experience
Pay More Attention to What Your Gut Intuition Tells You

I'd like to talk for a moment here about one of the biggest mistakes of my life, a man who shall remain nameless. He was a very attractive guy, wearing very attractive clothes, standing in very attractive surroundings. But when he started to speak to me, for a millisecond my gut flashed warning signs: "Stop this, get away, run and hide. Leave right now. You know he's wrong for you. What the hell are you doing? No! Don't you do it! Don't give him your number." But did I follow my gut?

I told myself it didn't matter, that my gut might be wrong this time, although I knew that to be the biggest, fattest lie I had ever told myself. Let's be honest here—gut or no gut, who would tell Mr. Perfect to get lost at "hello"? This guy exuded a gilt-edged charm that left me spellbound.

In truth, I didn't really expect him to call me. I assumed he checked me out, asked for my number, and chatted me up as part of his standard getting-to-know-you package. Even though I felt that his slick approach reeked of insincerity, my protests were weak, and I gave him another chance to wear me down. Do you know any guy who doesn't love a challenge? I managed to keep him at bay through two more calls until his final ultimatum surfaced: "Do you want to go out with me or not?"

I kept asking myself why I was making such a big deal about one date. He wasn't asking me to move to the Middle East or give up sugar. It was just a drink. His question hung in dead air space until I answered with an unconvincing, "Sure. Why not?"

Was I kidding? The little voice in my gut screamed at me: "Wake up, missy! You already know how this will end." But my mind was made up, and I didn't want to be confused by common sense. I told the voice, "You're wrong. I know what I'm doing this time." It was a big mistake.

Learn to Listen to Your Inner Voice

Any woman who is trying to find her way through the dating jungle needs to know how to listen to all the signals that she is sending herself. Her head, her heart, her hormones, and her gut are all chiming in and giving her advice. When you first meet somebody, you are probably hearing all this advice and reacting on a variety of different levels.

Your head, for example, may be running through a list of the new guy's qualities, saying things like, "He seems like an appropriate match: he's talking about things that interest me, he seems financially stable, he likes his work."

Your hormones may be coming through loud and clear: "I'm so seriously attracted to him."

Your heart is probably also chiming in: "I don't know him well enough to feel love, but I'm a loving woman, so I could probably fall in love with him."

Your gut is also advising you, but how do you recognize what's it's trying to say? When I tell people to follow their gut, I am telling them to follow their intuition. We all have intuitive responses. When we meet a new person, we can tell whether we have a genuine, positive human connection. We can tell whether something about this person is making us nervous. When a single woman who is searching for love meets somebody new, it's very easy to ignore what her gut intuition is telling her. She allows her head ("He seems like an appropriate match") or her heart ("I'm ready for love") or her hormones ("Wow!") to take over. In short, she doesn't always listen to that nagging little voice that says, "Wait just a minute. I don't know what it is, but something feels wrong here. I'd better either slow down or walk away now."

You don't need a medium or a psychic to give you important information about the people you date. Time and time again in my own life, I have had an intuitive gut feeling or sensation about a new man. It can be anything from a prickly feeling to a cold sweat. When I have failed to listen to that reaction, I have almost inevitably ended up in a troubled relationship. When I talk about this with my friends, they all say the same thing. You have to learn to trust your gut, because it doesn't lie to you.

Here are some suggestions:

- If you feel something isn't quite right when you meet somebody, trust your gut intuition. It's warning you for a reason.
- Don't fight those gut feelings. If you do, you may regret it in the long run.

- Wanting to see the good or positive in others is an admirable trait. But if you sense that the negative outweighs the positive, trust that reaction and move on. Remember your list of non-negotiables. You can sense some of them during a first meeting.

If you are a woman, you will probably face the following problem at least once in your life: You meet a super attractive man, and you are super attracted.

Your gut intuitive reaction is screaming, "Walk away! Watch out! This is trouble!" But entirely different parts of your body are also screaming, "He's so cute! How much harm can it be to just see what happens! Let's just see what develops. *I want him!*"

In short, you are being tempted to pay more attention to the signals your hormones and your crotch are sending out than the strong warnings your gut intuition is sending your way. Be careful and don't make that kind of mistake.

4

Me at Thirty—Why Am I Still Single?

It's an extraordinarily beautiful spring day, and I am standing on the dance floor of a large catering hall located on the bay in Howard Beach. The space is well known locally for its exquisite decorations, and today nobody is disappointed. I am surrounded by everyone in my family, along with at least two hundred other people. We are all patiently waiting for a glass elevator to come up through the dance floor. It does! And there she is: my beautiful sister. She is wearing an elegant white column gown and carrying calla lilies. How do you describe perfection? She looks like a top model in the pages of a high-fashion magazine; she fulfills every bridal fantasy. Looking at her, I see the happy glow on her face, and I start crying. So do many of the people around me.

It goes without saying that my sister's wedding was not the first I ever attended. By the time I had turned thirty, both my brother and sister had been married for several years. I was a bridesmaid for my brother, wearing an emerald-green gown, and maid of honor for my sister, wearing black velvet. Crying at my sister's wedding had nothing to do with any unhappiness about how I looked. My gown was lovely. In fact, most of my tears at Jolene's wedding were tears of joy. Later, at home, when I was alone, I would allow myself to indulge in some crying that had more to do with feeling sorry for myself.

Until Jolene got married, both my sister and I continued to live at home with our parents. Why not? It was extremely comfortable. My parents gave us all the freedom we needed to live our own lives, and the refrigerator was always filled with good things to eat. My mother prepared wonderful meals, always welcoming us, along with any friends we wanted to bring home.

My brother moved out into his own apartment when he was nineteen, but he still usually showed up for meatballs at Sunday dinner. My parents were incredibly supportive, kind, and loving. I was certainly never lonely. Living at home while my sister was also there was a lot of fun, even when one or both of us were going through sad times. We laughed, talked, commiserated, and hung out together all the time. Coming home after her wedding, I knew how much I was going to miss her. Of course, she was my best friend, and we would still talk and do things together—but it wasn't going to be the same, and the house was going to feel very different. That was at least one of the reasons why I cried.

But many of my tears had to do with larger issues. The wedding itself reminded me that I was still single, and I couldn't understand why. It had always been assumed among my friends that I would be the first to get married. Growing up, I had no fantasies about living the life of a single career woman; all my dreams were about having a family and sharing a life with one man. The only questions I had about marriage had to do with finding the best person and when it was going to happen.

I had a list of qualities that I wanted in a husband. Just to name a few, I wanted him to be my best friend and great with kids. Ideally, of course, I wanted him to be Italian like me. At the very least, he should be somebody who loved Italian food and wanted red sauce on everything. By the time I turned thirty, however, I realized that I might have to change my game plan. It was starting to dawn on me that my future wasn't going to be entirely based on what I wanted. In my twenties, I felt as though I was in charge, but by the time I turned thirty, the fact was that I simply didn't feel as though I had the same control over my life that I once had.

When I was in my twenties, the world seemed to be filled with eligible, cute guys who wanted to take me out. But during those years when I should have been dating dozens of men trying to find my future mate, I made a big mistake: I went from one serious relationship to another. I was always faithful to these men, and I never really dated anyone else.

Then, guess what? By the time I hit my thirties, many of the good guys were gone. They had been grabbed up. I remember one man in particular from college. He had a big crush on me, and I really liked him—but of course I didn't go out with him, because of Ken. After David and I broke up, I was struck with an impulse to try to find out what happened to that guy from college. Well, you know what happened to him: he got married, moved to the suburbs, put in a swimming pool, and had children.

While at my sister's wedding, I remember watching her have the traditional father/daughter dance. They looked wonderful together, but I have to admit I was a little envious. My father was a great dancer. So is my mother. At every event, they were always the best dancers on the floor—samba, rumba, cha-cha, they did it all. They could even waltz.

I adored my father, who often called me Butch. I never knew why, but when he used this nickname, it always made me feel loved and special. When I was a very little girl, I remember being at a cousin's wedding and dancing with my father, with my small feet firmly planted on his shoes. It was entirely possible that this was the time when my dreams of having a father/daughter wedding dance began.

I was very young when I started looking at bridal magazines and imagining my dress. It was so classic! I couldn't have been more than six or seven when I started dreaming about the large Cinderella princess ball gown that I would wear as I walked down the aisle on my father's arm. I couldn't actually see the man who would be by my side as I joyously exited the church under a sea of confetti and rose petals, but I knew we were going to be madly in love.

My parents, who had a very traditional view of marriage and family, encouraged my views. My mother had a very old-world upbringing; she was the only girl, the youngest child, with four older brothers. Her immigrant mother spoke Italian most of the time and was never really comfortable with English. My mother was very much the adored baby girl, but there was no question that my grandmother's household revolved around "the boys."

From a very early age, my mother learned that old-fashioned Italian women catered to their men. She watched her mother clean, iron, and cook. My mother was raised to be a pampered Italian American princess and an old-fashioned Italian wife, and she never complained about that role.

I should mention here that after immigrating to this country, my grandfather, Lorenzo Caputo, became quite successful. He started his professional life delivering ice door to door as an iceman. He started a jewelry business and a bakery shop. Later, he founded a fuel-oil company that became large and well known. Through all this, he never let go of his ties to his native Italy and was recognized for his donations and charitable acts to his Italian hometown. When my mother turned sixteen, for example, my grandfather took her to Italy for a sweet-sixteen birthday party and invited four hundred people from the community.

My grandfather was also a devout Catholic who never missed mass and was instrumental in building and maintaining the local church. In 1952, Pope Pius XII awarded him the decoration of the Knighthood of St. Sylvester, which I know everyone considered a really big deal. My grandfather died unexpectedly when he was only fifty-eight. When he died, his role in the Italian American business community was such that his congressman read a long piece about his life and accomplishments on the Congress floor, and his death was placed into the *Congressional Record*.

After his death, my grandfather's business holdings automatically transferred to his sons. It was assumed that my mother's husband would take care of her financial future. On some level, I think it always bothered my mother that the boys got the business, and I think my awareness of this is what eventually made me want to succeed as a businesswoman and be generous to my family and those around me. At least part of my motivation was to do it for my mother.

My mother is younger than Betty Friedan, who is often credited with starting the feminist movement, and the same age as political activist Gloria Steinem, but my mother was relatively untouched by the women's movement. There are no examples of bra burnings or women's marches in her history. She grew up in an age in which women essentially had three career choices: teacher, secretary, nurse. These were jobs that women were expected to hold only until they married. My mother went to secretarial school and worked as a secretary for a very short time before meeting my father.

When my parents met, my mother was twenty-one, and my father was twenty-eight. They met at the beach when my mother was struggling with her umbrella, and my father raced over to help secure it in the sand.

Coincidentally, it just so happened that relatives had arranged a blind date for the two of them for that very night. My mother learned this when her niece pulled her aside at the beach and said, "Aunt Bea, that's your date for tonight." For their date, they went to dinner at a restaurant in the Empire State Building and later rode the elevator up to the very top.

They were engaged within six months and married within the year. As a couple, they had very clear-cut roles. My mother's job was to be the homemaker; my father's was to go out and make money.

My father grew up in Yonkers with a Polish mother and an Italian father who wanted to be sure that he had a chance at a good education. My dad was especially proud of his Italian heritage and liked to tell us that we were descended from the Medici family, Italian Renaissance royalty. His parents sent him to a private military school and then college, where he earned an engineering degree. After college, he joined the army and basically traveled the world for at least two years.

By the time he met my mother, my dad had gone through what he referred to as his "wild" period, dating other women, and as a result, he was much more sophisticated about the world than his new bride. He also had a business in plumbing, heating, and air conditioning in the Bronx, both commercial and residential. Those were good years for this kind of business, and my father's primary concern was providing for his family so that my mother could be a stay-at-home mom.

I admired and looked up to my father. It always seemed to me as though he could do anything. He was an outdoorsman and sportsman. Around the house, he was the acknowledged expert on everything. He could build anything, fix anything, do anything; he even made furniture. He always stressed honesty, integrity, and a strong work ethic. He was also a devout Catholic and the head usher at our church. An extremely devoted family man, my father made us breakfast every Saturday and Sunday morning, taking orders the night before for what we wanted. All my friends developed small crushes on him because he was so handsome and debonair, with the most beautiful blue eyes.

In many ways, my sister, brother, and I had an idyllic childhood. We lived in a comfortable four-bedroom house on Long Island, and we had a summerhouse on the beach, thirty minutes away. We belonged to the local country club, and when we weren't swimming in the sound, we were in the club pool. My father and mother both cared deeply about animals, and we had a succession of much-loved pets.

One Christmas soon after my grandmother died, a beautiful golden retriever showed up in our yard. We immediately decided that grandmother had sent this dog. We named her Lucky, but her nickname was Nonni in my grandmother's honor. We never could find its original owner, and Lucky Nonni became a permanent part of the family.

I remember large Christmas Eve feasts of the seven fishes and equally large Christmas Day celebrations with my various Caputo uncles and cousins. And before you ask, yes, I am related to Theresa Caputo, the Long Island Medium. Her husband, Larry, is my first cousin.

My mother and father both liked to travel, and we would regularly go on family trips, sometimes with friends. In St. Thomas, I remember getting a bad sunburn and hanging out with a donkey named Natalie Wood. On that vacation, we were nine people crammed into a small hatchback, riding through the streets, singing "Show Me the Way to Go Home," which was one of my father's favorite songs.

In our day-to-day activities, though, my parents were relatively strict. When we did something wrong, we knew my mother would tell my father, and we would be in trouble when he came home from work. My mother is the kind of person who speaks her mind, no matter what. She is completely honest and can be relied upon to tell it like it is, but when it came to disciplining her children, she depended on my father to play the heavy. My father developed good relationships with all my boyfriends, but nonetheless he always made it very clear that he wasn't going to let anyone mess with either of his daughters.

The other thing that was a constant in my childhood was the Catholic Church. We went to religious instructions and mass once a week and went to confession several times a year. I took confession very seriously and would sometimes confess to things my friends did because I was sure I was also guilty. When I was about nine, I was in a supermarket with my mom and was so hungry that I secretly took a plum and ate it. Of course I went to church and confessed. The priest said, "Tonia, this is not that huge a sin—just realize that you can't take things without asking."

"But you don't understand," I cried to the priest, "I didn't wash it!"

My mother had always been so firm in her instructions about washing fruit that I honestly didn't understand which was the bigger sin—taking the fruit or eating it without washing it.

So my question is: given my background, with its emphasis on marriage and family values, why wasn't I married? After my sister walked down the aisle, I began to think even more about this question. The time had come to get serious.

Tonia's Tips:
Learn from My Experience
Don't Blame Yourself; Do Take a Realistic Look at Yourself and Your Relationship History

Women who are trying to explain to themselves why they are still single tend to veer between two extremes. One minute they are blaming themselves; the next they are blaming society and the men they meet.

Blaming—whether it's yourself or others—will not help you improve your relationships. What could help is taking a long, hard look at how you have behaved with men. This is not about blame; it is about getting more information as well as gaining greater awareness. Take some time. Think about your past relationships. Do you have any self-defeating patterns that should be changed? Have you learned from your experiences, or do you keep making the same mistakes over and over? It's really important that we all become more aware of our own patterns. We need to ask ourselves whether something we are doing, saying, or even wearing is attracting men who have qualities that are the exact opposite of those we want.

Ask yourself some questions:

- Do you have a history of getting involved with all the wrong men? For example, do you sometimes gravitate in the direction of unavailable men? By "unavailable" I mean men who are already in other relationships (or even marriages) or who live at great geographic distances.

- Do you have a pattern of letting relationships develop so quickly that you haven't spent enough time figuring out whether this is the right or the wrong guy? When you first meet a guy, have you asked questions that will help you honestly evaluate whether you share values and are on the same page?

- How about your attitude? Does it need some adjustment? As we get older, sometimes one of two things may happen: we either begin to feel desperate about our chances at finding a good relationship, or we develop an "I'm fine on my own" attitude. When you want desperately to be married, there can be a tendency to come on too strong and scare off potential mates. But if you go the other direction and don't make an honest effort, the people you meet may sometimes feel that you don't care. Try to stay somewhere in the middle. Don't play the excited, overeager puppy dog bouncing around looking for love, but on the other hand, don't be the indifferent, lazy feline lounging on the couch.

- Think about how you act once the relationship gets off the ground. For example, do you try too hard to please men? Do you do this so much that you are actually smothering? Or can you best be described as a high-maintenance woman?

In my personal relationships, I have to admit that I have always had a tendency to try to please the men in my life. I cook for them, I cater to them, and I tend to defer to them in the decision-making department. I don't do any of this in my professional life. Perhaps my instincts as a pleaser come from being raised in an old-fashioned family. Many men say they like their women to have these traits. But is this really true? Time and again, we see men take advantage of women who are accommodating, while catering to their more demanding, high-maintenance friends. If you have a history of relationships in which you have been much too eager to please, it might serve you well to learn to modify your behavior.

Or perhaps you are naturally a more high-maintenance person. The men you meet might eventually become exhausted from catering to your demands. If you want your relationships to improve, you also may need to make some behavioral changes.

It's important that we take a realistic view of ourselves and the attitudes and behaviors we bring to relationships. Sometimes, we can check ourselves by asking people we trust. If you have any really good friends who you know are always on your side, you might want to get their opinions. Before you do this, however, I'd like to remind you that you have to be absolutely positive that you won't become upset by or defensive at anything they say. You don't want to hurt your friendships.

Consider some Counseling or Therapy Sessions

If you have a history of one or more problematic relationships, you might also want to see a counselor or therapist for some sessions in order to honestly evaluate your romantic choices and dating patterns. This could help you gain greater clarity about how you have behaved in past relationships, what kind of role you played, and why the relationships haven't worked out the way you hoped. You need to honestly ask yourself some questions. For example, do you have self-esteem issues that are keeping you from making healthy choices? When it comes to men, are you attracting the exact opposite of what you say you want? Are you ignoring good men because they don't match unrealistic ideas of what is attractive? Do you give your heart too quickly? Are you making enough of an effort to find the kind of man you want?

Therapy can make a real difference in your life. People who get into accidents don't hesitate about going to physical therapy to help them recover. If any of your past relationships have resembled or felt like train wrecks, some emotional therapy or counseling could really help you heal and move on.

5

Let the Dating Games Begin

At thirty, when I looked back at my relationship track record, it seemed kind of depressing. Ken, Joey, David—three important relationships that bit the dust! Why was I still single? And what was next? The time had come to get serious. The challenge appeared relatively straightforward: I never had a problem getting dates, but was I getting the right dates? I was determined to become more organized and go the extra mile. If I did that, I was positive that I would be able to find my perfect life partner—my Mr. Right. One thing I knew for sure: I wanted to avoid wasting time on extended relationships that weren't going to work out for the long term.

My friends and family told me that there had to be some better matches for me out there in the dating pool. I agreed. Because I like to think that my approach to life is practical and methodical, I mapped out a game plan. What could I do to meet the right man?

Well, I did it all.

The Dating World

The women of my generation are sandwiched between two dating worlds: the old-world approach based on our parents' and grandparents' traditional way of forming relationships and the newer and more contemporary style, ruled primarily by the bar scene and the Internet. For some of us, this has not been an easy or simple transition.

When I was growing up, I expected that I would follow the traditional approach, which came with a clear and precisely drawn roadmap. The path went from living at home with your parents, to romance, to formal engagement, and then to the final destination: marriage, a shared home, and children. Dating was viewed as a defined prelude to a permanent relationship, not as a long-term chosen lifestyle. Casual dating had negative connotations, and, for the most part, it was avoided. Unmarried couples didn't travel together, and they certainly didn't live together. And let's not forget that the methods of birth control available to my parents' generation typically also meant that when young couples broke the rules and had sex, almost inevitably the woman became pregnant.

My mother and her friends were intentionally encouraged to maintain a limited view of the world—a little like putting blinders on a horse for its own safety. They were pointed straight ahead to avoid confusion and worldly swirls of distractions. Using my family as a reference point, they stuck to the safety of familiar faces and surroundings. Families hung out on the block—at the movies, the beach, the local church, and the butcher shop. When it came to meeting and dating men, my grandmother and mother followed the traditions of generations that had preceded them.

Like so many other women in my age group, my head was filled with romantic notions of how I was going to meet the man I would marry. I honestly expected that the magical day or "enchanted evening" would come when I would walk into a room, my eyes would lock with those of a perfect stranger, and we would both somehow know that we were destined to spend eternity together. I remembered hearing the stories about how my parents had met, when my dad helped my mom with her beach umbrella. I honestly anticipated that the same kind of thing was going to happen to me. By the time I turned thirty, I reluctantly had to relinquish these ideas.

In recent years, the dating world has changed drastically. Today, meeting the perfect mate is no longer left to fate. Instead, it has evolved into a big business. I know what I'm talking about. Not only can you expect to spend time, you will also spend money.

Friendship and the Single Life

Single women need girlfriends. They need other women with whom they can talk, laugh, and share experiences. Most singles can identify with the problem of returning home from a terrible first date—one of those evenings that make you feel as though you will never meet anyone and will always be alone. But when you have a good friend to call—one who will commiserate with you as well as help you see the humor in the situation, it all gets better.

When I started out on my quest to find a good man with whom I could build a solid future, I was fortunate because I was part of a group of romantically unattached single women of approximately the same age who were all doing the same thing. I realized I wasn't alone. My friends and I spoke often, and we supported each other as we made our way through the dating world. Looking back, having fun with my friends was probably the best part of being single.

"You never know where you will meet someone!"

That's what my mother said when she convinced me to become part of a weekend spiritual renewal program at our church. I thought it was a goofy thing to do, but my mother, who was tired of hearing me complain that I wasn't meeting the right kind of men, talked me into it. She hoped that I would meet a man from a good family who shared my values. Instead, I met Lorraine, another single woman, who shared a similar background and values. Lorraine, a blue-eyed blonde schoolteacher, never had trouble meeting men, but she didn't want to settle. She had broken off a couple of engagements, and like me, she was having trouble meeting the right kind of guy.

Lorraine and I quickly became sidekicks in our exploration of the single world. We were often joined by Susan, another pretty woman with a kind heart and large, expressive eyes. Once again my mother was instrumental in our meeting. My mother, who knew Susan's parents, fixed us up. When we went out together, we were frequently joined by a group of other single women.

Laurie was a successful attorney and another friend of Lorraine's who sometimes went with us. Laurie, an athletic, slender brunette who spends more time at the gym than I ever did, was always enthusiastic and outgoing and encouraged us to try new things. Another close friend of mine, Madeleine, a striking redhead, was incredibly dependable and reliable and always ended up taking care of everyone. I loved her because she always had my back. Whenever something went wrong in my life, I could depend on Madeleine to be supportive.

For the most part, my friends and I agreed: the number of ways to meet a mate are endless, and if you don't want to stay single, you have to explore every possibility.

Here are some of the ways we tried:

The Bar and Club Scene

I remember going to a half-dozen bars and clubs hundreds and hundreds of times. Thinking back, I can see myself very clearly. I'm in a bar restaurant on Huntington Harbor called Coco's Water Café, and I'm sitting on a barstool. The restaurant's most striking features include a wall of windows facing a panoramic water view. There are two bars inside, and in the summer, there are two more bars outside. During the summer, the outdoor bar area at Coco's was always mobbed.

The old Coco's no longer exists, but it had good and reasonably priced food. At 9:00 p.m., the tables from the restaurant were cleared and opened up to a dance floor. Typically, the music at Coco's was '80s freestyle, disco, with some rock and roll. The important thing is that there was always music, and everyone would dance. It seemed as though everyone was nicer and happier while dancing.

Walking into Coco's, my friends and I were usually dressed to the nines, prepared to have a good time. When I looked around, I would see approximately a hundred singles. At first glance, it might appear depressing, because there were probably three women for every one man. My friends and I were always in the bar area. We knew that a group of women sitting together at a table could appear intimidating and might make men less likely to approach us. For the most part, my friends and I were all different physical types, so we didn't think we were competition for each other.

We had certain routines about when to go to these places. Happy hour on Fridays after work were often good. So were Thursday nights, because Thursday is usually a big night for singles. And then, let's not forget Saturday nights. Although Saturday night is the traditional date night, it's also a good night to just hang out with your friends and dance. My sister met her husband at a bar/restaurant during happy hour, so I knew that it was within the realm of possibility—but I also realized that it was highly unlikely. Nonetheless, I tried to maintain a positive attitude.

When I train salespeople, I always tell them, "Expect a yes, but be prepared for a no." That was my attitude. I told myself, "Even if you never meet a guy this way, you can always dance!" And I love to dance! My friend Steven used to come to the clubs with us. He would sometimes drink too much and get loud, but by the end of the evening he was always friends with all the girls at the bar. And he's a terrific dancer.

If you go back to any of these places more than a few times, you will quickly discover that for the most part, it's the same old regulars, week in and week out. You get to know the bartenders and the rest of the staff. You see the same guys; you see the same women. It doesn't take long before you know everybody's history. You find out that "Pete over there in the corner" used to date "Sharon, who always wears the same Capezios," but that they had a friendly breakup. You discover that Neil has been divorced twice and met both of his ex-wives this way. Every now and then, a new person walks in, and that person could be Mr. or Ms. Right.

In my many years of dating, I went out with about five guys whom I met while hanging out with the bar/restaurant/club single crowd. I don't think any of my friends did much better. But we did have a lot of fun, and that counts for something. I should add that we didn't limit ourselves to bars or restaurants on Long Island; we often drove into New York City. More people—same results.

Summer Shares

In New York and New Jersey, and I'm sure throughout the country, singles have another way to meet people while also getting some fun in the sun: they rent shares in houses with other singles in communities that cater to the single summer crowd. My friends and I did this regularly. One summer we rented a cottage on the Jersey shore, but most of the time we were on Long Island in a town called Sag Harbor, which is loosely considered to be part of the Hamptons. I had other friends who preferred some of the beach communities on Fire Island, a barrier island located off Long Island's south shore.

The summer routine went something like this: on Friday afternoons, I would pack a few cute bikinis and some stylish clothes for the evening and head out to a house that I was sharing with four of my closest friends and another twenty-five or so people whom I didn't know so well. One year, my four friends and I shared a room with five slightly uncomfortable beds lined up across the room. There was no walking room whatsoever. To get to the bathroom, you had to jump over the beds. Our bedroom happened to be right near the front door, so we would hear all the drama that was going on. We knew firsthand which of our housemates were getting drunk and acting like jerks. There were so many people in that house that some of them were even sleeping in the basement, with sheets hanging as space dividers.

There was always a fair amount of mild bickering about what kind of food to put in the refrigerator, and there was never enough space for everybody to store their favorite brands of beer or hard lemonade. But we had many great barbecues; everybody would chip in money, and somebody would do the food shopping. That somebody was often me. My friends and I ate breakfast together—usually egg sandwiches that the least hungover of us would run out and buy at the nearest deli.

Once you got past all the inconvenience, you had a couple of days to enjoy yourself. The houses themselves were very nice, with large pools and tennis courts. Saturdays and Sundays were spent partying with everyone either by the pool or at the beach. In all the houses I shared, there was always one really hot guy all the girls drooled over. Our big question: Who was going to get him? Year after year, we received the same answer: the girl with the most cleavage and the most determined approach got the hottest guy—and it wasn't any of us.

At night, there were either parties or time spent at the local bars and clubs with hundreds and hundreds of other singles. Sundays, we would stop by a bar on the Montauk Highway. Then we would either drive home later, after the traffic had subsided, or early Monday morning before rush hour. Remember, we were still young and energetic. By the end of summer, I had a great tan, met dozens of new people, and had more than a few first dates. Did I ever start a serious relationship with someone? No. Did any of my friends? No. Did anyone I know meet anyone this way? Not really. One of my friends met a guy she dated for a while, but nothing serious came of it. While we certainly heard stories about people who waltzed off the beaches and headed straight to the altar, it just never happened to anyone I knew.

Speed Dating

Let's say a few short words about speed dating, which is exactly what it says it is. Two people speak for a few minutes and then decide whether they want to get to know each other better. For a few years, speed dating was all the rage, and many people I know tried it. I did it twice, with my friends Lorraine and Susan. The first time, we went to a speed-dating event on Long Island. None of us met anybody, but we weren't completely ready to give up on it, so we went to an event in New York City, hoping that the men there would be more our type. They weren't, but we might have just been there on the wrong nights.

The speed-dating phenomena actually has a bit of a scientific basis. Studies have shown that both men and women believe they *know* within the first thirty to sixty seconds of meeting someone whether they have any interest in pursuing the possibility of a relationship. Speed-dating companies base their business on this assumption that first impressions count for everything and getting to know a person counts for very little.

I remember all of the women being seated at one of twenty or more small tables arranged in a circle. Men, in the meantime, went from table to table introducing themselves. You got to talk to each of them for just a few minutes. What do I remember? It was a blur of tall guys, short guys, medium guys, stocky guys, thin guys, and strange guys. I remember guys with huge masses of curly hair and guys who were balding. Most of them were polite.

My least favorite question: "So why are you still single?" The implication seemed to be, "You're an attractive woman, so what's wrong with you? You must be high maintenance."

The men who sat down in front of me typically seemed to have a well-practiced opening line. It goes without saying that I will always remember the stocky, slightly balding guy who sat down and asked, "So do you wear grandma underwear or thongs?"

My answer: "Well, you are never going to find out."

There were men with a variety of different professions. I remember meeting a math teacher, a science teacher, and a lawyer. I didn't meet anybody I wanted to know better, but within a few minutes I was willing to take a good guess as to why each of them was still single. One guy, for example, had filthy fingernails. I would have given him a pass if he told me he was in construction, but the fact that he was a dentist totally turned me off.

After the event, there was time to mingle, and if you wanted to get to know somebody better, there was an opportunity to exchange information.

After both of the speed-dating events, my friends and I just wanted to get out of there and go someplace where we could have a glass of wine and something to eat together. Talking about our experiences was always both depressing and fun.

Dinner Clubs For Singles

Take four to eight single men and four to eight single women who don't mind spending money for dinner. Put them together in a moderately (or even extremely) expensive restaurant, and see what happens. These dating dinner clubs are found in most of the larger cities. They typically advertise that their members are attractive, intelligent, and successful foodies. Some of them advertise specifically for the over-forty crowd.

I've known people who really enjoyed these arranged dinner parties, so I decided to try it. I like food, and I also like intelligent, attractive, and mature men. I tried it only once.

I was seated between a psychiatrist whose office was on Manhattan's Upper West Side and a struggling freelance writer, also located on the Upper West Side. The writer and the psychiatrist were old friends, and they kept talking over me, mostly complaining about their ex-wives, ex-girlfriends, and what they were forced to pay for private school for their kids. I couldn't help wondering why they were spending so much for dinner if they felt so strapped financially. They had both been divorced for several years and already seemed to have a long dating history and no interest in settling down again.

I should also mention that in my particular group, most of the people at the table already knew each other, so I didn't really understand why they were there in this arranged setting. Maybe they really were more interested in the restaurants and the food than they were in meeting new people. I did end up talking with a woman I liked, and if I had wanted to make more women friends, this might have been a way of doing so.

The restaurant was way over on Manhattan's West Side, and I had to drive home to Long Island. I bolted before dessert, only to be blocked by the hostess.

"You can't leave yet," she said. "We haven't finished the event."

I apologized, but I told her that I really had to get home.

I like meeting new people, and the "arranged dinner party" might have worked better for me if it had been a slightly different group. I didn't come away with anything positive, but that doesn't mean it couldn't work for someone else. I truly believe that if singles don't want to remain single, they must explore every possibility—and the possibilities, along with good restaurants are endless. Someone wiser than I am said, "You hit what you aim at, and if you aim at nothing, you will always hit it."

Matchmakers

Calling a matchmaker certainly made me feel a little bit desperate, but I was determined to try it all. The new breed of matchmaker typically comes with a hefty modern pay scale. They package their services as a convenience for busy people, promising to save you time by separating out the true gems from the cubic zirconia.

The matchmaker's service is similar to that of a personal shopper. You tell matchmakers what you want, and they do their best. The personal shopper might discover a great dress, but you still have to try it on and hope it fits. Now, every woman trying to buy an outfit for a special event knows that the odds of finding what you want on the first try are slim to none, and we're only talking about a simple dress.

The disadvantages of using a matchmaker are obvious: it can be very expensive, and the choices they offer are typically limited only to their client pool, other people who paid them for the same service. There are exceptions to this rule, because some high-end matchmakers do extensive searches looking for Mr. or Ms. Right for the highest paying clients.

Despite my huge reservations about spending money, I made an appointment with a matchmaker. At that time, with this particular matchmaker, two or three dates would have cost me a few thousand dollars, but there are matchmaking services that can cost as much as a hundred thousand dollars a year or more. I ended up not signing up, although the matchmaker assured me that she knew the perfect man for me. He was a part-time comedian and a regular guest, appearing on a New York–based radio show that specializes in gross humor. Not for me.

I do have a friend whose father insisted that she try a matchmaker, which he paid for. This particular matchmaking service had all its clients create short videos, which other clients could then view. My friend did get a few dates out of this process, but none of the men seemed to be her type, and the process ended up holding little interest.

Some people do meet, fall in love, and end up marrying people they meet through matchmaking services. But others end up unhappy, sometimes complaining that the services failed to perform as promised.

Internet Dating

In the realm of relationships, Internet dating falls into the "new frontier" category. In this day and age, most singles have at least dipped their toes into these uncharted waters where sharks, always hungry for new prey, abound—even in shallow water. Talk to anyone who has signed on to any online-dating service, then pull up a chair, get comfortable, and expect the unexpected. The Internet is unregulated. It's the Wild West, with no sheriff in sight to protect you.

I signed on to Match.com, Plenty of Fish, and eHarmony, and used them off and on over a couple of years. Several of my friends were also trying Internet dating at the time. We spent a reasonable number of hours talking to each other about editing our profiles and choosing photographs to post online. I actually knew people who met people they liked on the Internet, so I believed the potential for success existed, but what are the odds?

Recently, I read about all the people who lined up to buy a ticket for the Mega Millions lottery. Their odds for success were a cool million to one. They had a better chance of being hit by a flying bus than they did of taking home that big prize. Did anyone care? Even I spent a few dollars, because the dreamer in each of us needs to reach beyond today. I also had some hopes for winning out on Internet dating, but it didn't work for me.

Internet dating sites do provide a legitimate service at a reasonable cost. The web-based services that I used operated with fair business models and didn't entangle prospective daters into complicated payment schedules with hidden fees. I don't hold the dating sites accountable for the lackluster results forwarded to my inbox. Their computers scan and impartially sort pages of information to match compatible applicants. How could anything go wrong? Computers calculate data without prejudice or emotion. The results must reveal the secret ingredient, the missing link to successful dating, right?

Theoretically, programmed matchmaking could work like magic if applicants were hooked up to a lie detector and shocked each time they fibbed as they filled out the forms. Unlike IRS computers that match new information against existing laws, online-dating services rely on the honesty of each applicant and determine results based on that data only. No matter how powerful or sophisticated the computer, it can't identify lies, nor will it intentionally tell lies. If the data fed into the program are false, the conclusion might appear correct, but it is not. The technology has been compromised not by the dating service or the computer but by the human factor—by those who are capable of telling the big lies.

Battle weary and armed with this hard-won information, I have culled a few possible scenarios from my scrapbook of Internet dating nightmares. Of course, you might avoid any mishaps and walk down a path that leads straight to the altar, like my friend Laurie, who ultimately married her computer match. Was it a true miracle, or did Laurie figure out the secret to dating online and writing a perfect profile? Laurie explained that instead of listing desired traits such as "tall, dark, and handsome," or favorite hobbies like "yoga and traveling," she got more in depth. She expressed her need for a deep emotional connection and focused on her core values, such as the importance of family life.

Laurie's experience demonstrates that anything is possible. Did I mention that one person did hold the winning ticket for the Mega Millions lottery and took home the whole prize? But if you log on in search of love, although there appear to be more success stories these days, you must still be aware of the odds.

Like many single people, I approached my first Internet dating encounter with high hopes but little in the way of real expectations. Surely this cutting-edge technology would distill the murky waters of dating not just into a gin-clear drink but a perfect martini with a twist.

When I checked my inbox after I submitted my first profile, the box was loaded. I was bombarded with too much information. What happened to computer screening? My list of potential matches resembled the choices on a Chinese takeout menu—endless. Was my profile so generic that it suited the needs of all these men, or had I hit the mother lode? Maybe I had inadvertently ticked the wrong boxes. My mind exploded with questions. I needed real answers. Wasn't that the primary reason I came to this site in the first place? I poured a glass of wine and took a look at the various hopefuls. It wasn't pretty.

Methodically, I sorted through the list. It didn't take very long to whittle down the group to a manageable few. I contacted my matches, exchanged additional information, and even met some on dates. For me, the circumstances always felt very stilted, but then I was new at this, a rookie. I thought I had worked the system astutely, but I wasn't getting anywhere, just treading water. Perhaps I was out of sync.

I called my friend Lorraine, who was an old hand at computer everything. She had recommended this particular dating site, so surely she would have answers, and she did. The next day I met Lorraine, and we analyzed my profile and my prospective matches: a printout of my unedited Chinese take-out menu. Suddenly, as we compared notes, she noticed certain undeniable similarities in the matches that we had both received. We had been introduced to the same people: the serial daters.

Eventually, I learned how to be more selective in replying to men I met on Internet dating sites, but it was an experience filled with trial, error, a little bit of discomfort, and quite a bit of humor.

How Did All These Dating Experiences Make Me Feel?

The process of trying to find an attractive and marriageable man sometimes made me feel as though I had embarked on a great adventure filled with unlimited prospects and a great deal of fun. Other times, of course, I felt like a total loser! Dating can take a terrible toll on your psyche. You have to be brave enough to reject good people just because they are not your type, and you have to anticipate being rejected in return. I certainly had my share of both.

Here's an experience I remember. Somebody I met on the Internet contacted me, and it turned out we lived near each other. Let's call him John. We made a date for drinks at a nearby steak house. Over drinks, it quickly became apparent that John liked me. He was very attractive, and I also liked him. I discovered that he was recently divorced and had two children. After about an hour, he said, "I'd like it if you could have dinner with me now. Is that okay with you?" It was more than okay.

We moved to a table in the dining room. John did the ordering—a good bottle of red wine, clams casino, a salad to split, a porterhouse for two, and creamed spinach. But when the food arrived, we were so busy talking and staring into each other's eyes that we barely ate anything. There was this gigantic piece of porterhouse going to waste. I was actually beginning to wonder why he was staring at me so hard. I went into the bathroom to check to make sure that there was nothing strange hanging out of my nose or sticking to my teeth. It was all clear. He just seemed to be very into me.

After a couple of hours of this, the server asked if we were finished. John said yes and gestured that the plates could be cleared. I'm Italian. In Italy there are even laws to discourage people from wasting food. I couldn't bear the idea of that happening so I asked, "Why don't you take the steak home?" He said no. I didn't say anything, but I knew we were talking about more than one hundred dollars' worth of grade-A prime beef. Finally, since it was apparent he wasn't going to budge, the server asked me if I wanted to take it home. I agreed to take a doggy bag. The server came back with the check. I really tried to get John to allow me to pay for half because I was taking home most of the dinner, but he repeatedly said no.

He told me that he would call me, but he never did. Looking back over the evening, I couldn't help but wonder what went wrong. He did most of the talking—about his marriage, his feelings, his kids, his work. In retrospect, I realized that he asked me almost nothing about myself so maybe he was very self-involved, and it was for the best that he never called.

But I still wondered why. Thinking about it, I remembered that his attitude toward me seemed to change when I agreed to take the porterhouse home. I know that seems ridiculous, but that's what I decided turned him off. He seemed to be so attracted to me, but when my hand closed around that doggy bag, he changed. What can I say?

Anyone who has dated for a long period of time, as I did, remembers many experiences that keep reverberating in our brains. You meet people, you spend intense hours hearing the stories of their lives, you laugh together—sometimes you even cry together. You begin to care about them. And then you never ever speak to them again. It's very strange. But it's very much part of surviving the dating world.

Dating definitely has its highs and its lows. Here's another evening I remember. For years, my friend Lorraine and I had a tradition: We would spend the Fourth of July weekend in Bayville, hanging out near the water, going to block parties, and watching fireworks on the beach. Long Island summers were a wonderful thing. But one year, Laurie told us that Bill, a fellow attorney and friend of hers, was having a party at his house on the Jersey shore. He implied that although he was married, there would be a lot of single guys there. We decided that we would break with tradition. Why not? Nothing ventured, nothing gained.

We made a reservation at a beachfront hotel near Bill's house, and the day of the party we started off expecting to spend no more than three hours driving there. We figured we would get there early enough to spend a couple of hours on the beach before going to his house. Well, the traffic was insane! It turned into a long, hot, seven-hour trip: getting off Long Island, crossing through Queens into Brooklyn, getting across the Verrazano Bridge, and then driving down to the Jersey Shore. By the time we got there, we barely had time to check into the hotel and change our clothes before it was time to hit the party, decked out in our best summer-casual garb.

The minute we walked through the door, we figured out what kind of party was taking place. Couples! Lots of couples! Everybody was married! I mean everybody! The men were grouped together talking about golf, sports, and work. Women, who all appeared to know each other well, were in bunches talking about work, home renovations, and their children. There were even a few children running around! If there were any singles in that crowd, we didn't find them. We stayed a couple of hours and went back to the hotel and found a beautiful spot near the beach to have drinks.

It was definitely some kind of cruel joke. All that effort and all those hours in the car just so we could end up sitting on the beach with a group of women. If I remember correctly, I think we actually started crying. And then, of course, we started laughing. At least we had friendship and each other. The next day, we headed back to Long Island with another crazy story to remember and share.

It wasn't long after that weekend that Laurie met her match on Match.com and went on to create her happily-ever-after life.

Tonia's Tips:
Learn from My Experience
Know What You Need to Know about Dating Etiquette in the Twenty-First Century

Dating has changed radically in the last twenty years. Before you agree to meet a new person, there are decisions and choices to be made. Where do you go? Lunch, brunch, drinks, coffee, dinner? What's the best kind of place to meet? When you do go out, who pays? Is it appropriate to tell your date that he missed the mark at the end of the evening? Should you call, text, or e-mail that you are no longer interested? Is ghosting ever appropriate?

Dating is supposed to be fun. Here are some suggestions to help you keep it that way and avoid unnecessary trauma:

Think about Where to Meet
I prefer a casual place. Meeting in an informal setting for drinks or a cappuccino at a coffeehouse removes at least some of the stress. If you do like each other, it's easy to go on to dinner or make plans to meet again. On the other hand, if it's apparent that you and your date have no future together, you can both walk away amicably and avoid suffering through an expensive dinner and dessert. Simple always works best.

Don't Drink Too Much
First dates can be nerve racking. As we get older, tension and nervousness at the idea of meeting someone new may

become even more intense. Some people are just sick and tired of dating; others have recently ended relationships and are upset at the idea of starting all over again. No matter what the reasons for stress, follow the usual drinking rules: one or two drinks at the most, and not on an empty stomach. Don't risk the possibility of a DUI; remember, usually any blood-alcohol content above 0.08 percent is reason for a citation. A woman who weighs 125 pounds and has two glasses of wine can quickly reach that level. Driving when legally drunk is dangerous and foolish. Also, don't forget what a DUI can mean in terms of not being able to drive your car for an extended period of time.

You're also old enough to know what happens to most of us when we drink too much. You may end up looking drunk and foolish, or worse—you may say something or do something that you will regret in the morning.

Save the Sex for a Later Date
When it comes to sex, many singles say, "I'm an adult, and I know what I'm doing." I completely understand that you are tired of being alone, and I understand why you might want a chance at ardent, passionate, loving sex. I'm not questioning the fact that you are an adult. I'm questioning whether you absolutely need to jump in the sack immediately.

Sex, if you didn't know, means taking off your clothes and seeing each other naked. And that is a huge step for two people who have just met. Real intimacy requires comfort and trust in one another. It's almost impossible to get anywhere near that point after a two-hour dinner or drinks at a bar. Try to get to know each other a little better. If you have sex too soon, it can interfere with getting to know the real person. Lust has a way of making us forget everything else, and that includes personal feelings.

Holding off on sex tends to make the other person even more interested, not less, and it allows the relationship to develop. If you are serious about wanting to find a real relationship, as opposed to a quick night in bed, don't be afraid that saying "no, not yet" will make a man lose interest. It will probably make him more interested. Besides, any man who doesn't understand "not yet" is probably not the person for you.

So try to keep the early dates PG rated, okay?

Limit Conversations about Your Romantic History

Let's face it, the chances are good that you've already been in several relationships and possibly even a marriage or two. It's normal to be curious about someone's past, and I'm sure you'll come across a date who asks about your history. Nonetheless, avoid talking about your ex or exes and the problems you had in the past. It doesn't matter how horrible your exes were; it doesn't matter whether they cheated on you, lied to you, or took the television set and dining-room furniture when they left. It also doesn't matter if they were wonderful, brilliant, or left a gaping hole in your heart. You definitely don't want to spend your first date (or dates) with someone new reminiscing about someone who is no longer in your life instead of getting to know the person sitting right in front of you.

Think about it. If you tell your date about how you and your ex would argue all the time, he may wonder if you initiated the arguing. If you tell your date you were cheated on, it may enter his mind that there was a reason for the cheating. Your past is your past. Focus on the present and your current date. It's okay to talk briefly about your history, but leave out the sordid details, regardless of your date's interest. You can share more after you get to know each other better. In the meantime, it's your personal life.

How about the Check?

Most experts agree that if a man asks a woman out, particularly if he has chosen the restaurant, he should pick up the tab on the first date. I've even read male dating experts who suggest that when a woman is adamant about paying half on the first date, she runs the risk of sending the wrong message—that she isn't interested in him and doesn't need any man. Gauge your reactions depending on the circumstances. If you're getting the message that he is really strapped for cash, don't suggest expensive restaurants or order the most expensive thing on the menu. Keep it modest.

The women I know don't mind paying their fair share once the relationship gets off the ground and understand that tight finances are a real concern today. Nonetheless, they typically say that if a date makes his frugality known by not even suggesting ordering an appetizer if they meet for drinks, then he is toast. I understand what they mean. I remember going out for first dates immediately after work.

We would meet for a drink around dinnertime, sit for an hour or so talking, and then nothing. Not even a stuffed mushroom or a small plate of roasted peppers and anchovies. I find it peculiar that these men asked me out again. This is not about the money, but something much greater. If a man is blatantly cheap about money, there is a good chance that he will be cheap about other things; he may be limited in his ability to give of himself in a relationship and, instead, be someone who withholds love, emotions, and compassion. This characteristic applies to both sexes and shouldn't be brushed aside.

Show Your Old-Fashioned Manners

I always appreciate men who open car doors, help you put on your coat, and take your arm when you cross the street. Etiquette never goes out of style. This is also true for women. Remember to say "please" and "thank you," and don't eat with your fingers. If you go to the restroom, excuse yourself when you leave the table. Be polite to the waitperson. Keep your voice appropriately modulated. Be polite up until the last minute of the date. It's rude to give up in the middle of the date and retreat into a sulk. See the situation through to the end. It builds character. Besides, a woman with class would never mistreat someone because she is bored or ready to go home. Does anyone remember class? Think Cary Grant or Audrey Hepburn.

Also, don't take over. Don't tell him what to order or tell him what to do. Men tend to dislike women who act bossy on the first date, or, even worse, act like their mothers. My male friends say that they respect strong women, but they don't need or want another mother. Assertiveness may work wonders at work, but a lighter, gentler hand will prove more effective with your dates.

Let Him Know Whether or Not You Are Interested

Unless a date is a total jerk, everyone deserves a second chance. First impressions are just that—impressions. People are generally nervous on a first date and may come off as boring, aloof, or lacking in humor. This can be caused by a simple case of nerves and fear of rejection. If you feel there was a glimmer of something positive that is worth pursuing, don't be afraid to do so. Subtly let him know that you are interested by thanking him for a nice evening and saying something simple, like, "I look forward to seeing you again."

If he doesn't call or text you within the week, it's apparent he is not that interested. But what if he calls and you are disinterested? Let's say you have been out twice, and you know there is no future. What do you do when he gets in touch with you? Some people avoid confrontation these days by simply ignoring messages. In the modern world, this is called "ghosting," and it's a recent dating phenomenon. Personally, I think it's impolite and really bad form to run and hide. Good manners dictate a level of sensitivity and a definitive response. If he asks for a reason, you can say, "I don't think we're a match, but it was a pleasure meeting you." Don't give him a long, complicated explanation about all the things you disliked about him; less is definitely more. A guy I once went on two dates with asked me out for a third time. I was honest and told him I felt we lacked romantic chemistry. We both agreed that we liked each other enough to hang out platonically and wound up becoming good friends.

6

Some Wonderful, Some Weird, Some Worse

We all have stories to tell. Women who have dated for more than a few years know that some men remain in our memory banks indefinitely, even if we only went out with them a few times or knew them only a few short hours. My friend Laurie, for example, can never forget Costco Guy.

Laurie and Costco Guy met at a party. He asked her if she wanted to meet for lunch the following weekend. Laurie, who is a very easygoing and agreeable person, said sure. He called Saturday morning and asked if she could meet him at his house. Laurie said sure. The first problem: traffic. It took Laurie an hour and a half to get to his house, where she found him waiting in the driveway.

"I'm starving," Laurie said as soon as she got out of the car.

"Not a problem," he replied. "I just have to pick up a few things at Costco, and then we'll go straight to lunch."

Laurie figured, why not? Maybe she could pick up a year's supply of hand soap or paper towels while she was there.

As soon as Laurie and Costco Guy walked into the store, he steered her in the direction of the sample food. He went from table to table, time and again fighting his way through groups of mostly white-haired shoppers to reach his goal of little cups of instant mashed potatoes, small tidbits of cheesecake, miniscule servings of Nutella, one-inch-square pieces of bread with hardened salami, and cheese, lots of cheese. A few times, Costco Guy scored two of everything—one for him and one for Laurie. But most of the time, he just stuffed his face with the one sample, smiled, and moved on.

After about forty-five minutes of this, Laurie said to him, "If we are going to go to lunch, shouldn't we be leaving?"

"You want to go out to lunch now?" Costco Guy asked. He sounded surprised. "I'm stuffed. I couldn't eat another thing. Saturdays here are always the best! My father and I have lunch here all the time."

Laurie had agreed to this lunch date because she assumed they would be able to sit down and talk so she could get to know more about him. But after an hour of watching him elbow the elderly to get his fair share of prized delicacies such as lime Jell-O with pineapple morsels, she figured that she knew enough. "You're right," she said. "I don't want anything else. I just want to go home."

She stopped at the nearest deli on the way home to get a sandwich.

Some of the best stories in my life come from experiences with Internet dating. Let's talk about some of the people I've met and you may meet while dating in the twenty-first century.

The Compulsive Dater

The compulsive dater is basically addicted to dating. He dates everyone he can, without any plans to develop a more serious or intimate relationship. The goal is as many dates as possible. This person, who is often found on Internet dating sites, isn't interested in anything but variety and a feeling that he has unending options. Men who fall under this category are like breeding stallions. They tend to look for those women who are new to Internet dating in order to stable them for a future date. Compulsive daters are sometimes men who are recently divorced. They had a taste of commitment, and they don't want to try it again anytime soon. Compulsive daters are typically on several dating sites, and they are active on all of them. On first glance, compulsive daters can appear charming and agreeable, but once they are convinced that you are there as a future option, they tend to move on and get back into their dating groove.

The Trawler

A specific subset of the serial daters, these guys are particularly active on the Internet. It isn't news that there are more single women than men on dating websites. Trawlers take advantage of this situation, moving from site to site just to see who is out there. Trawlers want the endless buffet, and their dates either don't know or don't care.

I once asked an active trawler if his number one girlfriend, Ms. Weekend, knew about the other women he was dating. "Why would that matter?" he replied. "When I'm with her, she gets all my attention."

Is this really what the world is coming to?

The Texting and E-mail Expert

This may just be me, but I find that men who have no interest in allowing the relationship to grow beyond texting or e-mail communication are particularly annoying. I've known men who give really great e-mail. A common technique is to send e-mail after e-mail baring their souls while delving into yours. At first, this approach can be very engaging. Writing back and forth, particularly late at night, tends to create a false sense of intimacy and trust. But be wary: some of these people don't ever want anything to become real. Even if you meet, you may discover that your greatest conversations and time spent with them is on the Internet and not in person.

I remember an exchange with someone I met on a dating site whom I assume was a guy—but who knows, since we never met or even spoke on the phone. After we exchanged several dozen e-mails and texts over the course of a couple of weeks, I finally asked.

"Why don't we have a real chat, on the phone?"

His response: "We will as soon as we meet in person. I don't know you well enough yet."

My return text: "Do you have a timeline?"

"Not sure yet."

"Wouldn't you prefer one phone call instead of spending all this time texting?"

He didn't respond, so I tried again.

"Couldn't we accomplish more with one conversation?"

He answered: "Maybe, but I'm not ready to talk."

I like games, but this one was too stupid to continue.

My final text: "Have a nice life, whoever you are! Don't contact me again."

The number of people who can't get beyond texting appears to be growing. Some of them can text faster than the speed of light. One can only hope they are not doing it while they are driving.

Some possible reasons why texters and e-mailers stay hidden behind their computers, tablets, and phones might be that they are married, underage, or, at the minimum, playing games with your head. There is no reasonable explanation for the person who doesn't want to have real communication, so my instincts flash red warning lights. If someone doesn't want to have a phone conversation or meet with you, that usually spells married, some kind of con, or serious emotional problems. (See section on "Catfisher" below.) Something is wrong! This relationship is doomed, and you will only end up with calloused thumbs and more texts. My advice would be to take this very seriously and shut down all further communication.

The Catfisher

By now, just about everybody knows that a catfisher is someone who posts a fake profile on the Internet with the hope of luring in unsuspecting and often naïve men and women who are looking for love and romance in all the wrong places. This doesn't just happen on reality TV. Catfishers are known for their ability to keep unsuspecting people involved through the art of wireless communication. Avoiding real meetings is an efficient way of making certain that you will never discover their true identities. I have to say that I don't think I've ever been catfished, but it's happened to people I know. If you are dating on one of several Internet sites, for example, it's probably very easy for somebody to post a false profile. There is no guarantee that the photos you see are real and connected to the person with whom you think you are connecting.

Catfishing doesn't happen only on Internet dating sites. I met at least one woman, Clare, who had the sad experience of discovering that she was engaged in an online romance with a woman passing as a man. Clare, a recent widow, was on a listserv site that was technically set up for caregivers, which she had been for her late husband. She was contacted off list by someone who said his name was James; he described himself as a man who fully understood the stresses of her life because he had been through much the same thing while caring for his late wife. He told her that he lived two thousand miles away. Within a short time, Clare was deeply involved in an online communication with him. Clare and James exchanged long, intense, emotional e-mails. When Clare suggested that they Skype or use FaceTime, James always had reasons why he couldn't do that. Clare finally figured out that something was seriously wrong. It turned out that James was really a woman living in the same state. For Clare, this was a devastating and traumatic experience that sent her to a therapist.

The Stalker

Just last week, my friend Donna told me that one of her best male friends, a recently divorced forty-five-year-old, was now dating women he met on the Internet. He was also stalking them. His computer know-how, combined with a job that gave him access to a large number of databases, provided him with skills that most of us don't have. When he goes on an Internet dating site and sees the profile of a woman he thinks he might find interesting, he is often able to do enough research to discover her name and address. Then he goes and hangs out in her neighborhood, watching her move about her life. If he finds her attractive, then and only then does he attempt to make contact through the dating site. Donna is shocked. She can't believe that a man she has known and liked for many years would resort to this kind of creepy behavior.

I met my first stalker (let's call him Gary) soon after I signed up for Internet dating. He wrote to me. I looked up his profile. He seemed cute and appealing. We exchanged e-mails, we spoke on the phone several times, and we made a date. I was still sufficiently inexperienced about this kind of thing that I ignored the common advice of never giving anybody your real name. Everyone says the same thing: "You don't want strangers to be able to find out more about you, particularly where you live." But, as I said, I was still pretty trusting. In my naïve head, I thought, *Hey, we've talked on the phone a few times. He's not really a stranger.* Mistake!

After some back and forth, Gary and I agreed to meet on a Friday night. That morning I woke up with a sore throat, high fever, and a terrible headache. Before I crawled back into bed, I e-mailed Gary, saying that I was really sick and could we reschedule. Within the hour he called me back.

"What makes you think you can do this to me?" he asked with a snarl.

"Do what?" I asked. "I'm sick. I think I have the flu." But even as I said it, I was beginning to see the light about this guy. He was, as they say, nuts!

"Look," I started to say, "this is a big mistake. I don't know what you think, but I really feel sick and have to get off the phone."

He launched into a full-scale rant. "You can't do this to me. You can't get away with this. I know where you live, so don't be surprised if you see me drive by your house."

"If you do that," I warned him, "don't be surprised if I call the police."

Remember, I didn't know what he looked like in person, and I certainly didn't know what kind of car he was driving. His words made me a little nervous, but I probably didn't really take him all that seriously. However, within days it became apparent that there was one specific car that was regularly circling the block I lived on and often parking across the street from my house. He was making good on his promise. I made good on mine.

The police officer I talked to reiterated the same advice I had heard before: "Don't give strangers your last name. It's too easy for somebody to figure out where you live. And somebody you have recently met on the Internet is definitely a stranger, no matter how attractive he may appear." During this same time frame, my friend Steven moved into my house for an extended stay. When he saw the parked car, Steven confronted the guy. He told him that I had talked to the police, and we now had his license number, and he had better stay away.

It took a few more interventions from Steven before the stalker moved on. Through this experience, I discovered that it is not a crime for someone to drive around your neighborhood or wait for you in dark places. Technically, you can't take any legal measures unless the stalker does something illegal. Meeting on the Internet doesn't count.

The False Advertiser

Just about anyone who has ever done any Internet dating has met at least one person who bears no resemblance to the photo or profile listed on the site. I always remember the man who I think of as "Surprise! I'm the real Robert!"

One long summer afternoon, I decided to try a new dating website that catered specifically to my age group as well as location. I filled out the necessary form and got a quick response from a man who, on paper, matched everything I had listed. And, let me tell you, his photo looked great! I began to think that maybe, with a little bit of perseverance, this Internet dating might work out for me. He called and suggested a trendy restaurant known for its elegance and gourmet food. What a gentleman! I was psyched!

First dates with someone you think you might like take time and money. I went through the usual ritual. I got my hair, nails, and toes done so I could wear strappy sandals, consulted with friends about what to wear, chose an outfit, and walked out the door with all the confidence of a celebrity heading for the red carpet. At the restaurant, a valet opened my car door and another uniformed person opened the door to the restaurant. As I walked in, my eyes immediately started to scan the bar area. No one looked familiar, and my little brain raced with possible scenarios. Maybe Robert had changed his mind or was stuck in traffic. I could feel tiny little beads of unhappy perspiration form around my hairline. Just what I needed—a halo of sweat framing my makeup.

The tuxedo-wearing maître d's deep voice broke through my thoughts. "Miss, are you looking for someone?" I smiled and asked if Robert had arrived. He pointed to a large, balding man sitting at the far end of the bar, holding a huge bouquet of red American Beauty roses.

I smiled as I could feel my teeth go into a serious clench. "Of course," I lied. "There he is. How could I have missed him?" *Holy mother of God*, I thought. Who was this man? *Maybe Robert couldn't make it and had sent his best friend to apologize.*

Either I needed glasses, or this was some terrible mistake. "Robert," I said in my softest voice as I approached the man holding the roses.

"These are for you, hon," he smiled.

Then I spotted another little package tied with a satin ribbon sitting next to his glass of bourbon. I could feel everyone at the crowded bar paying attention to the little drama that was unfolding before them. I didn't know where to hide. My face remained frozen, and not because of any Botox. I was just stunned by the man who handed me the roses.

I took a long hard look at the Real Robert, who had already begun reciting the unabridged story of his life. He didn't even stop to notice that I was speechless. I would never have recognized this man from his photo. I would kindly estimate that his profile took more than fifteen years off his age, and these years had robbed him of the thick hair and ripped abs that were prominently featured in his profile photo. Robert, who strategically balanced his girth on the barstool, was dressed beautifully and had great manners. But he had misrepresented too many factors.

Believe me, I'm not a hard woman. I could have accepted the receding hairline, the extra pounds, or even the additional years. But put all these elements together, and they spell dishonesty. What else had he neglected to tell me? This was not a good way to begin a relationship. Needless to say, I never went out with him again.

The Completely Unexpected

Once you enter the dating world, I can guarantee that you will come in contact with problems that you couldn't even begin to anticipate or imagine. You are inevitably going to meet people with all kinds of emotional issues, and they may well get you involved in their own personal psychodramas. In this category, I had several dates with someone I think of as Suicidal Sam. My experience with Sam was sufficiently upsetting that it sent *me* into therapy.

He and I met through an introduction at a local club. He was with another man who was described as his cousin and best friend. Sam and I went out several times over the course of a month. He was a nice guy, but he really wasn't for me. After a few dates, I told him I thought we were both better suited for other people. He seemed to agree.

Yet a few weeks later, my phone rang at midnight. It was Sam. He told me he was holding a bottle of sleeping pills and a bottle of Scotch, and, he informed me, he was permanently "checking out." And, guess what, it was my fault. Click.

Fortunately, I remembered his cousin's name and was able to track down his phone number. Shortly after midnight, I called him to tell him what Sam had said and asked him to do something quickly.

"Don't worry about it," his cousin said. "He's done this before. Trust me, he's not going to kill himself. Forget about it, and just get some sleep."

Well, I thought about it a few minutes and realized that I couldn't forget about it. I had nobody else to call, so I called the police. And it was a good thing I did. They broke down Sam's door to discover that he had followed through on his threat. He was hospitalized and put in a psychiatric facility. And I needed a shrink to help me handle my guilt.

I couldn't help but blame myself. I kept thinking about what happened between us and worried that I had done something wrong. What did I do? What did I say? What didn't I say? Maybe I hadn't been honest enough. Maybe I had led him on.

I found seeing a therapist very helpful. He assured me, "This is not your fault. Chances are, this is not the first time he has done this. Yes, this is a call for help, but you are not responsible."

It's important to remember that when you are in the dating world, the people you meet have real feelings. Although I ultimately came to see that Sam's over-the-top reaction to a little bit of rejection was not my fault, I learned a real lesson about the importance of sensitivity.

A couple of years after this incident, I learned that Sam was getting married to someone. It made me feel very happy and relieved.

The Professional Liar

Men in this category simply don't want to be pinned down. You can sense that you are not getting the whole story (which frequently includes a wife or another girlfriend), but you can't be absolutely certain what's going on.

I've certainly gone out with more than a few men who fit into this category. I've also met men who lied about what they did for a living or who spent an entire evening trying to convince me how important they were. Why were they pretending to be something they were not?

Stories abound about con men who try to take financial advantage of women they meet on the Internet. I don't think that I've personally met one of these men, but I know they exist, and I realize women need to be very cautious. If something about a man's story seems strange, you need to check it out before letting the relationship move forward.

Another man I remember because I nicknamed him Lying Lloyd. A plastic surgeon, he was one of my mother's favorites, because she thought he would fulfill her fantasy of a lifetime of free medical advice and plastic surgery. If truth be told, I instinctively knew that I wouldn't end up with him, but my friends were so impressed with his credentials that I wanted to give the relationship a chance and continued to date him for the wrong reasons. When I broke up with him, everyone was disappointed—except his ex-wife, whom he had been still seeing, along with the old girlfriend who was the primary reason for his divorce.

Tonia's Tips:
Learn from My Experience
Stay Safe

Back in the day, my friends and I were told that we should always have our dates, particularly first dates, come to the door to pick us up. These days, of course, we women are typically advised never, ever to let men we don't know anywhere near our front door.

If you believe that dangerous situations happen only to other people—those you see on the news—you're not being very smart. When dating men who are complete strangers, it's essential that you proceed with caution. As far as your physical safety is concerned, here are some easy rules to follow.

- If you are using any of the popular dating sites, be careful about posting anything that would make it relatively easy for someone to find out your basic information—last name, address, phone number. Remember that if someone has your phone number, it's possible to do a reverse lookup and, in this way, learn your name and address. This is now true of cell phone numbers as well as landlines.

- I would suggest getting a new e-mail address to be used specifically for dating. This way, if you find yourself in an uncomfortable situation with someone you met, you can change your dating e-mail address without having to notify everyone you know. It goes without saying that this e-mail address should not include information that would allow someone to find out your last name.

- Also, don't create any links between dating sites and social media, which would enable strangers to learn more about you. Don't post photos with anything that will help identify you, such as a picture of yourself standing next to your car with your license plate showing. Restrain yourself and don't give guys you meet any of your basic information except your first name until you know more about them. As careful as you may be, we are all learning, privacy is becoming more and more limited these days. Protect yourself as best you can.

- If any of the men you meet seem at all creepy or weird, trust your gut intuition and stay away. But also remember that sometimes the nicest-appearing guys can turn out to be whacko and/or dangerous. Remember, you are not a mind reader. You have no way of knowing for sure what is going through the head of the person sitting across the table.

- The first time you meet someone, do so in a very safe public place. Continue to do this until you know much more about him. And don't agree to meet anyone in a parking lot.

- At the end of the date, go home by yourself. Don't let him drive you or escort you or do anything that will give him access to your home address until you know him better.

- Always make certain that you are carrying a cell phone with a fully charged battery. Make certain that at least two close friends or family members know where you are going to be, and have a firm plan that you will be getting in touch with them by an agreed-upon time.
- If you have anything to eat or drink, keep your eye on it. Remember, date-rape drugs are odorless and tasteless. Don't leave your drink sitting on the table when you go to the ladies' room.
- Be careful about leaving your purse or wallet where your date can access personal information.
- If anything about your date seems strange, pay attention and think twice before agreeing to spend more time with him. If, for example, he is overly vague and isn't willing to give you some detailed information about who he is, watch out.
- Don't immediately take his word about his name, address, phone, or marital status. In this modern world, you can easily check many things, so do your fact checking. Also, if he doesn't exist on the Internet, consider the possibility that he has given you false information.
- Make sure that you are carrying some cash and a credit card.

- Some experts suggest that you carry pepper spray or mace (if it is legal where you live). When I first started dating, my protective father gave me pepper spray, along with instructions on how to use it.
- Once again, don't drink so much that you are not in control.
- It goes without saying that it's not wise to go to his home until you know much, much more about him.

Physical Safety Isn't Your Only Issue

Dating can feel very scary. No matter how you meet someone, whether on an online-dating site or through an introduction, you are exposing yourself. We all know what it is to come home from a first date feeling as though there is no hope and you will never find someone to love. I also don't know anyone who hasn't felt hurt and rejected—and most of us have probably ended more than one date feeling that we have said or done something extraordinarily stupid. Dating is filled with emotional and psychological risks. If you meet someone really wonderful, you will feel as though it is all worth it. However, understand that meeting that someone may take a lot of time and emotional energy. So here's some advice.

- It's unlikely that you are going to meet the right person on your first, second, third, or possibly even the twentieth date. Don't take it all so seriously. Just try to have fun, and while you're at it, you can learn more about yourself and the world around you.

- Be kind to the men you meet.
- Don't do anything that you will later regret: Don't post any over-the-top photos of yourself on social media. Don't write any overly intimate e-mails. Don't share information about yourself that you will later wish you hadn't. Absolutely *do not* indulge in any sexting!
- Don't become obsessed with someone you just met. Don't think too much about what "he's" thinking or doing and don't start planning a future together in your head.
- If you know that you have a tendency to open your heart too quickly, have some counseling or therapy sessions before you start dating so that you can become more aware and learn how to avoid old behavior patterns.
- Know and respect your boundaries. Don't let your boundaries drop just because this guy, who you just met, starts saying things you have always wanted to hear.
- Protect your emotions and don't assume that when a man asks you out several times he wants a serious relationship.
- Take each date as a learning experience. Not everyone will be for you. You will be disappointed, and you will also disappoint others.

Most Important!

Be true to yourself. Stay centered and aware. You know the core you and what you value. Don't push that aside just because some guy is persuasive and you're lonely.

7

Long Term Doesn't Always Mean Forever

Yes, relationships take effort, but when your interactions with a romantic partner begin to require more work than a full-time job, it's time to rethink your situation. Life is hectic and exhausting enough without being in relationships that require repair on a constant, day-by-day basis. Here's one of the most important lessons that single women need to learn: *know when it's time to let go.*

I understand that this is not always the easiest thing to do. When you are in a romantic relationship, strong emotions create confusion; it's not always so easy to coolly assess the situation and take action. Ending unsatisfying or even unhealthy relationships can sometimes take a lot of courage.

I was single for more than twenty years, so it stands to reason that I had more than my share of relationships that lasted more than a few months. They often started for a reason that many single women will recognize: I wasn't being careful, and

I paid more attention to attraction than I did to common sense. And they ended for reasons that most of us will understand. Here are some of my most notable longer-term relationships.

He Was a Serious Drinker

Okay, let's admit it: Andrew could easily be described as an alcoholic. But I didn't know that when I met him. I just thought he was an attractive, charming guy who was a great deal of fun. I probably should have noticed that most, if not all, of our dates included a lot of alcohol, but at that stage of my life, his behavior didn't seem as extreme as it does now in retrospect. When we went out, Andrew ordered cocktails before, and at least one bottle of wine during, dinner. After dinner, he preferred Scotch. I certainly couldn't keep up with him, and I didn't try. I don't like feeling as though I am out of control, so I would purposely limit how much I drank. This sort of annoyed him, so I would sometimes try to hide the fact that I wasn't drinking as much as he was.

Andrew also appeared able to hold his liquor. Nothing about him screamed out "drinking problem." He had a demanding job at which he was successful; in fact, his job, which required a fair amount of social drinking with clients, probably contributed to his problem. But the rest of his life seemed very normal. He had family as well as dozens of friends who loved him. He could hold his liquor and never appeared to become overly drunk or inebriated. At least not at first.

We were at least six months into the relationship and things between us were starting to get serious before I noticed that Andrew wasn't holding his liquor quite as well. When we were together in the evening, he appeared to be getting sloshed on a regular basis. And he was starting to get angry. At me! Over small things that made no sense! I could see that his alcohol intake was contributing to his problems with anger management, and I begged him to cut back. And he did, for a week or two. Then he quickly returned to his old pattern.

When you are with a drinker, there are other things that are troubling. I would worry about his driving, for example. On the nights we weren't together, I would wait for him to call to tell me he was home, so I wouldn't have to think about his safety on the roads. Sometimes I worried about going places with him, because I was afraid that he would make some kind of scene over something small and stupid. At family parties, I made sure that we didn't stay that long, so that he didn't have a chance to drink as much as he might have. I certainly didn't want my parents—particularly my father—to notice that he could get out of control.

While I knew him, Andrew was becoming more and more successful. He was a young guy on a high, and I was there right with him. I'm not perfect, and I would like to admit that during that period of my life I had my own drunken-stupor evenings. But we were definitely not in the same league. I really cared about Andrew—and let me say that I was prepared to change our lifestyle and stay away from bars and clubs if he would agree to it. I tried to convince him to go to AA, and he may have attended a few meetings, but he didn't want to admit there was a problem.

We had a great deal in common, and we really enjoyed being together when he was sober. But our relationship quickly turned into a roller-coaster ride of his stopping and starting the drinking. And when he was drinking heavily, he was becoming less and less charming. On evenings that he drank heavily, he would go on ego trips, telling me that he was "the best" this and "the best" that. When he drank he also started becoming inappropriately jealous. Once in a restaurant, for example, he became convinced that I was flirting with someone a few tables over. He said, "I saw you checking that guy out." Trust me, I hadn't even noticed the guy, but I couldn't convince Andrew of that fact.

I would also like to add here that I heard rumors suggesting that Andrew was not being completely faithful to me. For example, a woman he worked with told a woman I knew that they were going out. It really upset me. I confronted him, but he denied it. Sometimes you let things go because you don't want to know the truth. I think this was one of those times. It took more than a year, but we finally broke up after a fight in which he began calling me names. I don't even remember why, but of course he had been drinking. We were standing together on a shiny tile floor. He pushed me. I was wearing high heels and went flying.

I couldn't believe that this happened—and I couldn't believe that I was in a relationship in which this kind of thing could happen. I loved him, but it was time to end it. It was painful, but I had to admit that we were not going to be together for the rest of our lives.

This experience taught me to be more aware of how new men in my life handle their liquor.

He Was Addicted to Porn

Porn is changing the nature of male/female relationships. I had certainly heard about men who were more interested in what was taking place on their laptops than they were in pursuing genuine intimacy. However, I probably didn't believe it was real until I went out with Dennis.

We met on the Internet, so I guess it was appropriate that we should break up because of it. Dennis was an interesting guy. And very smart. And very attractive! And we really got along. When I met him, I thought, *This could be serious.* We went out for several months before I couldn't help but notice that Dennis wasn't even trying to become more intimate. What was with that? At first I thought he was being respectful; later, it started to seem weird. If I was at Dennis's apartment, by nine o'clock he would be hinting for me to leave. If he was at mine, he would begin yawning and moving toward the door even earlier. Who ever heard of a guy who never at least tried to spend the night? There must be an explanation.

It goes without saying that I blamed myself. Perhaps Dennis didn't find me attractive. But then why, I would ask myself, was he continuing the relationship? I also wondered if he had some kind of a physical problem that he wasn't sharing. Maybe there was a medical issue.

I discovered the reason when he made the mistake of leaving the apartment with his computer open. Yes, Dennis was addicted to porn. It was apparent: given the choice of spending time with me or with dozens of enticing women on a computer screen, the women on his laptop won out over the woman on his lap. Since my time with Dennis, I have heard almost identical stories from other women. There seems to be an epidemic out there.

My friend Tina told me that she ended her engagement to her fiancé, Greg, because of his porn addiction. Tina thought Greg was a little strange because he never wanted to sleep over at her apartment. She discussed it often with her girlfriends. They thought that it was possible that Greg was immature and became anxious about being away from home. If she and Greg spent the night together, Greg always preferred that Tina stay at his place. On those nights, she would often wake up in the middle of night and see a light from the living room. It was Greg on his computer. She would ask, "What are you doing, hon?"

"Just checking invoices for the business," he would reply. "Go back to sleep."

Checking invoices at 3:00 a.m. seemed strange, but Tina let it go. She was happy that Greg was a hard worker determined to make a success of his business.

There was one other weird thing about Greg that Tina began to notice: he would surreptitiously check out other women's boobs when he thought Tina wasn't looking. One day, her outspoken aunt called her aside and said, "I don't know how to tell you this, honey, but that guy of yours keeps staring at my cleavage." Tina was mortified. When she tried to talk to Greg about it, he told her she was crazy, not to mention insanely jealous.

Eventually, Greg asked Tina to become part of sex acts that made her uncomfortable. When she told him that she was sorry, but she would never want to be tied up, even with velvet ribbon, he became angry. At this point, she woke up to realize that something much more serious was going on. Yet Tina continued planning their wedding, acknowledging to herself and her closest friend that she and Greg would probably need to see a therapist as soon as they were married.

One morning, Tina and Greg were together at his apartment. They were expecting an important e-mail from Greg's lawyer regarding his divorce papers from his previous marriage. The lawyer called and told Greg to look at the e-mail. Greg opened his laptop so that he and Tina could look at the papers together. Afterward, Greg went to take a shower, failing to log off. Tina decided to check his search history. She had a difficult time restraining her tears. Greg's Internet search history was filled with porn.

At first, Tina was afraid to confront Greg, but eventually she did. He told her that a friend had sent him the sites as a joke. Tina knew he was lying, but instead of recognizing that Greg had a problem, she put the blame on herself. She thought he was turning to porn because she wasn't satisfying him. She went racing to Victoria's Secret to invest in some serious new lingerie. And she discussed the issue with her best friend, who told her to see a therapist, which she did. Tina ultimately realized that Greg's behavior had nothing to do with her and that Greg had a serious addiction. This wasn't behavior she wanted for the father of her children. She called off the engagement. Tina told me that she has no clue if Greg is still addicted but she believes that's what contributed to his divorce from his first wife.

When I started working on this book, I also interviewed a man named Tim, who confessed he started looking at porn at work. Porn became his lunchtime ritual, until his boss busted him two months into it. Although Tim stopped looking at porn at work, he continued to view it at home. He was not married and did not have a girlfriend. He told me that he really wanted to meet someone special but was sick and tired of going out and striking out. Eventually, he found himself simply staying at home and viewing porn sites until late at night.

Tim was smart enough to realize that porn was consuming his life, and he eventually went to therapy. After he kicked the habit, he would come home to an empty house and had difficulty not logging on to fulfill his fantasies. Tim told me that he wanted a normal relationship more than anything. Finally, he was introduced to someone he could see having a future with, and he wasn't about to ruin that. Today, Tim is in a committed relationship and chooses to stay off all social-media sites, since that's how he originally got hooked on Internet porn.

Just like any other addiction, porn addiction can wreak havoc on people's life. It can negatively impact productivity at home and at work, causing people to withdraw from or sabotage their relationships.

If you are a single woman, there is a very good possibility that you will cross paths with a porn addict. Porn addiction is also becoming more prevalent among women. Take a look at these statistics I found online about porn, which I'm sure are increasing as I'm writing this:

- Every second, 28,258 users are watching pornography on the Internet.
- Every second, $3,075.64 is being spent on pornography on the Internet.
- Every second, 372 people are typing the word "adult" into search engines.
- Forty million American people regularly visit porn sites.
- Thirty-five percent of all Internet downloads are related to pornography.
- Twenty-five percent of all search-engine queries are related to pornography, or about sixty-eight million search queries a day.
- Thirty-four percent of Internet users have experienced unwanted exposure to pornographic content through ads, pop-up ads, misdirected links, or e-mails.
- Of the e-mails sent or received every day, 2.5 billion contain porn.
- Every thirty-nine minutes, a new pornography video is being created in the United States.
- At a meeting of the American Academy of Matrimonial lawyers, two-thirds of the 350 divorce lawyers present noted that excessive watching of Internet porn had contributed to more than half of the divorces.

Probably the most important thing I can say to women who face this kind of problem in their relationships is that they need to realize that it is not their fault. It is not because they are not appealing or desirable. If you are involved with a man you believe to be a porn addict, try to get some professional support so you can sort it out for yourself.

He Was Gorgeous!

Franco was every woman's ideal of what an Italian man should look like. I called him "My Italian Stallion." We met at the drive-through Dairy Barn. At that time in my life, I was living in an apartment and every morning on my way to work, I would head to the Dairy Barn where I would roll down my window and order coffee and a roll with butter. I was still young enough so that I could have a roll with butter every day and not gain weight. I haven't had one of those rolls in more than ten years!

The Dairy Barn had a drive-through with two sides. It was amazing how often we would arrive there at exactly the same time. Franco and I would be rolling down our windows almost simultaneously. Was that fate or what? He started saying, "Hi. How are you?" I couldn't help but notice that he had a very slight, but thrilling, Italian accent. After several months of this, one day he got out of his car and asked for my number. It was like we practically knew each other, right?

I can't really explain why I went out with Franco. We would probably have been better as friends. Okay, let me admit the truth here: it was complete physical attraction. I thought he was adorable. And he was a nice guy. In the back of my mind, however, I always knew we didn't have a future together. It wasn't that we didn't have things in common. We did. We shared a serious interest in all things Italian, and I loved the fact that he was so into cooking and eating Italian-style meals. When I look back at the relationship, I certainly remember pleasant times. My mother thought he was "cute," and although she didn't quite understand the relationship, like me, she appreciated his interest in food.

When I met Franco, he had only been in this country a short time, and he was running the deli department in an upscale food market. He told me that his dream was to open his own market. I did whatever I could to encourage and further that dream. I would drive around with him to help him scout locations for his own business. By the time we stopped seeing each other, he owned his own deli, specializing in Italian food.

There were several problems with the relationship. The biggest was that he had very old-world views of a woman's role. I knew he was a great cook from visiting his store and sampling dishes like his orecchiette with broccoli rabe and hot sausage, but at home, he saw cooking and cleaning as being woman's work, so he would never cook for me. I didn't want to be with someone who viewed me as an old-fashioned Italian wife, tied to the kitchen and catering to her husband while he acted as if he was still single—which brings up the other problem with Franco.

I was pretty convinced that he was a player. You might remember all those old Italian movies with the devastatingly handsome Marcello Mastroianni, always incapable of fidelity, while his wife stayed home cooking the pasta. That's what I was afraid of. I finally told him, "We both know that we are better off as friends." He argued with me a little bit about that, but I knew that he knew that I was right.

With every failed relationship, I learned something. From Franco I learned how to make mozzarella from scratch and how not to burn my hands the next time. He was a good guy, and we stayed friends for quite a while. We were just not meant to be together long term.

He Was an Older Man

Everyone was telling me I was too picky and that I needed to start settling. I was close to forty, and I myself was getting scared. Perhaps I would never get married. Perhaps I would never have children. That's when I met Jeff.

By this time, I had my own house and had developed a new morning ritual. Every day on my way to work I would stop in Dunkin' Donuts and get a container of coffee. Some days I also ordered breakfast, usually an egg-white veggie wrap. While I was there, I often spotted a good-looking man who seemed to be staring at me. He had his own morning breakfast ritual: black coffee and a blueberry muffin.

One day when I was standing there giving my order, the counter person told me that my breakfast had already been paid for. He gestured to "Mr. Coffee, Black, with a Blueberry Muffin," who was now sitting down. I didn't want to make a scene just because some impeccably groomed guy had dropped four dollars and change to buy me breakfast, so I did the only thing that seemed reasonable. I walked over to his table and said thank you.

His name was Jeff, and he was attractive in a Sean Connery older-man kind of way. It didn't take Jeff more than a few minutes to tell me that he had been trying to figure out how to introduce himself to me, and that he really hoped we could talk and get to know more about each other.

Up front, let me also say that Jeff was one of the best-dressed men I had ever met. He always wore top-tier suits and shirts, and on his wrist, he was wearing a Rolex that I knew set him back more than a few thousand dollars. He looked and acted like a respectable, reputable, and successful guy. But when he asked me out, I hesitated, because he seemed much too old for me. I didn't want an older husband—even if he did look like Sean Connery. But he was a very persuasive guy, and I finally agreed to dinner. On our first date, he took me to a lovely restaurant; he was charming, attentive, fun, and interesting. He told me that he was ten years older than I was. He also told me that he had one child and that he was divorced. He said he was still living in the house he had shared with his wife, but she had moved out.

I still thought he was too old for me and didn't want to see him, but he kept calling. And when I discussed this with my friends, they all told me that I was crazy. "If everything else about him is good, ten years is no big deal!" was the common advice I got. I was very conflicted about going out with him. It just never felt right. But he always did things that made me feel guilty about wanting to break it off. One night, for example, we were walking through the mall, and I stopped in front of a store window for a second to admire a pair of shoes with a $900 price tag. "You have small feet, don't you?" he said.

"Not really," I replied.

"What size are they?" he asked.

"About a seven and a half," I told him, shaving my foot size a bit, because they are actually closer to an eight.

When we got to the restaurant, he excused himself to use the men's room. He was gone for a long time. When he returned, he was carrying a shoebox.

"I can't accept these," I told him.

He insisted that I just try them on, which I did. Fortunately, they were too small. I went with him back to the store and, over his objections, returned the shoes.

The next day, there was a package at my door. The shoes were there—size eight. Without the receipt, I had no way to return them so he could get the credit.

The primary message I'm trying to convey here is that he was incredibly persistent, which made me sense that he could be more than a little controlling. But there were several other things that also bothered me. For example, he never wanted me to come to his house, and he had a million excuses why. Finally, I Googled him and discovered that he lived less than ten minutes from me. Like millions of women before me and after me, I did a drive-by. It was a mansion, and there were several cars—as well as a woman in the driveway.

I asked him about the woman. He told me that although he and his wife were separated, she had yet to move out as planned. They were "not together," he assured me, but I didn't believe him. Within the same time frame, I learned that he was almost twenty years older than me, not ten, as he originally said.

It was all too much. It seemed obvious that I had to break it off. I said, "Listen, I don't think this is going to work, and I don't see it going anywhere. The age difference is an issue for me. The fact that you originally lied about your age is an issue. The fact that I've never been inside your home is an issue. The fact that you are still living with your so-called ex-wife, and I don't even know for sure if you really are separated, is an issue for me. It's all too much."

This was a man who was accustomed to having things go the way he wanted, and he had no intention of taking no for an answer. My friends kept warning me that he appeared to be obsessed with me. I don't know if that was the case. I do know that no matter what I said, he continued to call almost every day and show up on my doorstep without any warning. This went on for months. I happened to meet somebody who knew him in a different context. "Watch out," this acquaintance warned. "He has an obsessive personality. If he gets his mind set on something, he doesn't give up."

Finally, I told Jeff that I had started a new relationship. I thought that would convince him to go away, but it had almost the opposite effect. He got even creepier. One day he called and said, "I know you're dating a doctor who drives a BMW. I've had him followed, and he's cheating on you."

I remember screaming, "First of all, if you're paying a private eye, he isn't very good, because I'm not seeing a doctor, and the man I am seeing doesn't drive a BMW. Second, you're a psycho.

"I've talked to the police," I continued, which I had. "If you don't stop this," I said, "I'm going to file a report. You're a well-known, successful member of this community. You don't want something like this on your record."

I don't know whether that threat convinced him to go or he simply lost interest, but Jeff stopped calling, and I never heard from him again. It goes without saying that I always made sure that I went to a different Dunkin' Donuts to get my morning coffee.

He Was a Married Man

My relationship with Jeff was as close to a relationship with a married man as I ever got. Nonetheless, I realize I can't write a chapter about relationships that "have to end" without talking about married men in general. Certainly, I had several single girlfriends who had long, protracted affairs with men who were still married. Some of them started these relationships not knowing the facts, because the men lied and told them they were separated. In other cases, the relationships developed at work.

That's what happened with my friend Annie, for example. A successful lawyer, Annie worked for a firm that hired another lawyer, Ed, after she had been there for more than two years. She and Ed were assigned to work on the same case. They were overwhelmingly attracted. They were also working around the clock as well as traveling together. One night, while in a strange city after a long day of work, things got out of control. Annie was madly in love. Ed told her that he felt the same way and that he was going to leave his wife as soon as his youngest child graduated from high school. Year in, year out, Annie waited. She didn't look for another relationship; she didn't try to meet anyone else. After four years, the child graduated, but Ed never followed through. All of Annie's friends warned her that this might happen, but she believed in Ed, whom she described as her soul mate, and she believed in the relationship.

Recovering from this kind of betrayal and heartbreak is extremely difficult. The fact is that if you are a single woman, the best advice I can give is to not date or fall in love with a married man. It's inevitable that somebody is going to get deeply hurt, and there is a very high likelihood that you will end up being the person who suffers most.

We All Know Why Our Relationships End

Relationships end for a variety of reasons. Sometimes it's just a matter of timing, and one or both of you isn't genuinely ready to settle down. Sometimes, you just know in your gut that this isn't really the person for you. Other times, we end relationships because we're not being treated the way we want to be treated. You may love somebody, but you may feel as though your love isn't being fully reciprocated. In short, he isn't making you feel as loved as you want to feel. Many times we end relationships for concrete reasons: he may be lying; he may be cheating; he may be emotionally abusive in dozens of small ways; he may even be physically abusive.

When relationships end, it's important that you are clear about one thing: if you end it, you are doing yourself a big favor. If he ends it, ditto. You don't want to be in a relationship that isn't making you happy. Just be confident that you will find something better.

Tonia's Tips:
Learn from My Experience
Avoid the Ubiquitous Cheater

The odds of a woman entering the dating world without meeting a cheater are slim. She may discover that it's her trusted boyfriend, or she may fall victim to one of those guys with a great (and sincere sounding) rap, who can't resist trying to get every woman he meets into bed and succeeds as often as he fails. The difficulty is that men who cheat don't come equipped with large, flashing neon signs saying, "Watch out! Cheater on the loose!"

Recent surveys indicate that the level of cheating among married or committed couples has stayed about the same over the last decade. Really? Now maybe it's just me, having come across too many cheating men, but I think the results of this study could be a little suspicious. If cheaters regularly tell bold lies to their significant others, why would they suddenly confess the truth on this national questionnaire?

Probably the most memorable cheating story ever is one that made the rounds of Long Island after 9/11. Some say it's an urban legend, while others claim it really happened. Here's the story:

About a year after the towers fell, a group of Long Island women met for lunch. They chatted about the usual stuff until somebody mentioned 9/11. Vickie, a woman who was new to the group, suddenly teared up.

"My husband worked there," she said. She looked nervous, while the others waited in silence. Had they intruded into a sacred moment?

Vickie then told the following story: "My husband left home at the same time every day. After he walked out the door on the morning of 9/11, I took the kids to school and then came home to clean up the kitchen. The TV was on. When I saw the second plane smash into the second tower, I fell to the ground. That's where my husband worked. I started calling him at the office. Obviously, I couldn't get through. I called his cell phone. Nothing. I held onto the counter as I watched the towers fall. I cried harder. At some point, the doorbell rang. Both my mother and sister came to be with me. So did other friends throughout the day. All day long, friends came by, many of them bringing food.

"For endless hours, I redialed his number. And I kept redialing. Somebody picked up the kids from school. I didn't know what to tell them. Throughout that long morning and afternoon, I kept dialing his cell phone. After I watched the last building brought down, I remember burying my head in my hands. And that's where I was, surrounded by friends and family when, through my sobs, I heard my phone ring at about six o'clock.

"'Hello,' I answered.

"'What in hell is going on?' I heard my husband's voice asking. 'I have a hundred and twenty calls from you on my Blackberry.' He sounded furious.

"'Where are you right now?' I asked automatically.

"'I'm sitting at my desk, working. I'm about to leave the office. Where the hell do you think I am? Damn it, Vickie. I'm just trying to make a living!'"

By now, all the women at the lunch were transfixed by Vickie's story.

"He and his girlfriend, who was a coworker, had spent the entire day in her apartment having sex. Most of the people in his office died. I was happy he was still alive for the children's sake, but I never wanted to see him again. We got a divorce."

Another classic cheating story involves baseball legend Babe Ruth. As the story goes, while Ruth was still in bed with one of his many lovers, his wife arrived home unexpectedly. Shocked, she stood silently as the Babe uttered his denial—his girlfriend still next to him, clutching the sheets to her chest. "Who," he asked, "are you going to believe? Me or your eyes?"

Here's the thing you need to know about people who cheat: they are typically very good at it. They have very little guilt about what they are doing, and they are usually practiced liars.

So How Do You Know a Cheater when You Meet One?

When you enter the dating world hoping for long-term commitment and fidelity, I think it's wisest always to hope for the best, but be prepared for the worst. Many people—male and female—in today's world have problems with fidelity. The first thing to notice is how he reacts to other women when you are together. It's okay if he looks, which is a good signal that he is alive. But is he spending so much time looking that you get the sense that he is actually *checking them out*?

Getting a better handle on whether or not a guy is a habitual cheater is one of the reasons it's advisable not to go to bed with someone too soon. After you've known him for a while, you'll have a better idea of who he is and what's important to him. Nonetheless, if you are out on a first, second, or even third date, here are some questions you can ask and conversations you can have.

- In a casual conversation about the highs and lows of dating, you can ask him how many women he is currently dating. If he says anything other than "none," there is a good possibility that he is cheating on somebody. If he avoids answering the question, or appears to be lying when he answers "none," there is a good possibility that he is cheating on somebody.
- You can ask him why his last important relationship ended. If he says anything to indicate that infidelity on his part was a contributing factor, take this into consideration before getting any more involved. He may not say that he was unfaithful, but he could say something like, "I wasn't really ready for an exclusive relationship with her," or "She wanted more

than I could give." Answers like this are sending signals that he may not be ready for a committed relationship.

- If fidelity and commitment are important to you, don't be afraid to let him know that this is the case. If he seems to really like and be attracted to you, it's okay to ask him where he sees himself in a year. Is marriage and family one of his goals? Or does he want to spend several more years dating? Factor his answers into how you think about what is happening between you.

- Does he appear to have a great many women "friends?" Notice if he says things like, "I went to the movies with my friend Laura," and "My friend Sandi and I went for a walk in the park." It's normal for a man to have one or two good women friends, but few men have that many.

- If he gets phone messages, texts, or e-mails when you are with him, is it apparent that he doesn't want you to see them?

- Does he always ask you out in the middle of the week and never on weekends?

- Is he too practiced in the art of seduction? Does he immediately make you feel extraordinarily special? You may be enjoying it in the moment, but it could be a signal that he is good at seducing women.

- Does he seem to be concealing something? For example, is he vague about his plans? When you ask normal questions, does he make you feel as though you are prying?

- Is he secretive? Does it seem as though he wants to make certain you don't find out too much about his life? Notice, for example, whether he wants to include you in his life. If your relationship appears to be taking off, does he make plans for you to meet some of his friends?
- If you do meet some of his friends, do any of them say anything that can be interpreted as a warning? If so, pay attention.

8

Standing on My Own

Yes, I was out there, surviving the dating world, but I was also trying to maintain a grounded life with a semblance of normalcy. When I was thirty, with no husband in sight, I realized that the time had come for me to move out of my parents' house. I needed to rent an apartment. I was going to be the very first woman in my family to live on her own. It was a big step, and I felt very brave.

My friend Stephanie saw the ad for an apartment in the *Long Island Pennysaver*, a giveaway newspaper known for its classified section. She came with me to look, as did my mother. It was a one-bedroom apartment located in the upstairs of a house. The moment I looked at it, I knew I loved it. As far as I was concerned, it was perfect—cozy, homey, and very cute! I would live there happily for close to eight years. My landlords were a wonderful Middle Eastern couple, with grown children, who became like my family. They were so good to me. I appreciated the exotic cooking smells that would float upstairs from their kitchen as well as all the delicious food they would bring me as a special treat. I will admit that my clothes sometimes reeked of Middle Eastern spices, but my love of food outweighed any concern about lingering odors.

As soon as I signed a lease, I went shopping and bought a couch, two chairs, and a television. My brother gave me a stereo; my mother and sister went shopping to buy me dishes. My father not only bought me the right-sized kitchen table but also came over to put it together. My new queen-sized bed fit easily into my bedroom and joined the dresser and armoire that I took from my room at home. I was a single women who was finally living alone.

My first few nights in the apartment I felt a little nervous; I remember checking the windows and door a couple of times, but I fell asleep, secure in the knowledge that I was on the second floor, and my landlords were there in case of emergency. I should also add that I was paying a very reasonable rent. It allowed me to take trips, save money, buy clothes, and hang out in restaurants with my friends. The apartment wasn't really large enough for major entertaining, but it was big enough to be able to invite my family and friends over for dinner. Most Sundays, however, I still went home for my mother's meatballs.

Unfortunately, when I rented that apartment, I was also quite sad and somewhat depressed. I had just broken up with David and was going through yet another case of the breakup blues. To be honest, one of my strongest motivations in deciding to move out on my own came from a desire to protect my parents; I didn't want them to have to experience any more of my relationship ups and downs. The psychodramas of my single life had caused them too much unhappiness. They had been through enough, and I wanted to spare them.

I should quickly add that my parents were always there for me, even though I was living alone. I remember one Christmas Eve going to their house early to help prepare for the traditional Italian American Feast of the Seven Fishes. Together, my father and I opened up a fifty-pound bag of clams, which we were going to stuff and bake. While doing this, I must have eaten half a dozen raw clams. As always, we prepared a huge meal, and as the evening progressed, I ate large amounts of just about everything—appetizers, fish dishes, as well as a variety of pastas, not to mention dessert. By the time we left for midnight mass, I was starting to feel a little funny, but I was still okay.

It was after church, while I was driving home, that I realized that something was wrong—very wrong. I felt so sick I didn't think I was going to make it. But I did, just in time to vomit as I walked through the door to my apartment. I spent the next hour or so being violently ill in the bathroom. I was so sick, I was hallucinating. Instead of calling 911, which I should have, I called my parents. My always devoted father, true to form, drove half an hour at 3:00 a.m. He carried me down the stairs of my apartment and took me to the nearest emergency room. I spent most of Christmas Day in the hospital. I was the only person to get sick from our dinner, so I'm positive I ate a bad clam, and I ate it raw.

As sick as I was, I still couldn't help but notice that the emergency-room doctor was very cute. I remember saying to my dad, "Is that doctor as hot as I think he is, or am I hallucinating?"

"He's an attractive guy," my father replied.

"But he'll never look at me when I'm like this," I whimpered.

I got out of the hospital after 6:00 p.m. on Christmas day. I was so sick that I was home in bed for most of the next week. Two weeks later, friends and I went to Killington, Vermont, to ski. Never one to lose an opportunity, I remembered the doctor, who had given me his card to call in case of an emergency. "I'm going to call him and find out if he is single," I said to my friends.

I actually got him on the phone. "I don't know if you remember me," I said, "but I'm the girl who was suffering from food poisoning on Christmas Eve."

"Yes, of course," he answered. "How are you?"

"I'm all better," I told him, "but there is something I have to know. Are you single?"

"Well," he replied, "I actually just got engaged."

"Congratulations," I told him. "But if it doesn't work out, I just want you to know that I look a lot better when I'm not suffering from food poisoning."

He laughed.

That was probably the first and last time I ever called a guy I just met. In fact, I had a self-imposed rule that the man had to be the one to make the first overture—but, after all, some rules were meant to be broken at least once.

When I moved into my apartment, I was also in a relatively new job, working for a man named Walter. Once again, I was managing a sales team. As a manager, I had a small salary as well as an override on the sales in my room. The more my salespeople made, the more I made. If I wanted to be successful, I had to be certain that my salespeople did well. I had worked with some of the people at my job before. Others were new. When I first started there, I missed my friend Steven, who had moved to Arizona.

Most of the people I was working with were young and still single. We all had our dating stories to share. The women would tell horror stories and complain about the men they were meeting; the men would tell horror stories and complain about women.

I remember meeting Mark, another manager, with whom I became friendly. At that time, Mark was still single. He and our other male coworkers seemed able to match the women story for story. Some complained about women who were more interested in meeting men with money than they were in building relationships; others shared stories about women who behaved inappropriately or caused scenes. More than one guy had a story about being stalked. I always remember one of them telling us all about a girl with whom he made the mistake of becoming intimate, when he was young. He didn't think it was that serious, but she was determined that they were meant to be together. He was shocked when she confronted him and said she was pregnant. This was a good guy who wanted to do the right thing, so he talked to his parents. They also wanted to do the right thing, so they called a contractor and started making plans to put an addition on their house. They would help support the young couple and take care of the baby so that both of them could finish school. As this family made plans to upend their lives, the young woman finally admitted that she had made up the pregnancy story.

When I had questions about the men I was meeting, I often found myself going to my male coworkers, particularly Mark, to get the male point of view. Mark and I became so friendly that he felt like family—and we argued like brother and sister.

After a few years working for Walter, it became apparent to me that the time had come to move on. I loved the people with whom I was working, but as a boss, Walter wasn't as generous as he should have been. I made him quite a bit of money, and my sales team was outperforming expectations. Walter had promised me that if my team met a certain goal, he would give me a $10,000 Christmas bonus. We had more than matched that goal, but at Christmas, Walter seemed to forget his promise, and instead of a bonus he and his wife handed me a wrapped box from Nordstrom. Inside the box was a handbag with a Louis Vuitton label.

When I looked at the Nordstrom box, I was immediately put on guard; I said to myself, I don't think Nordstrom carries Louis Vuitton. It might be a fake. I remember Mark being more definitive. "That's strange," he said. "Nordstrom doesn't carry Louis Vuitton."

Soon after Christmas, I took the bag to the Louis Vuitton store in Manhasset's Miracle Mile. Perhaps I was wrong; perhaps it was real, in which case I wanted to exchange it for a different style. But I wasn't wrong. The salesperson at Louis Vuitton was quick to tell me, "This is an imitation. Where did you get it?"

I explained, "My boss and his wife gave it to me."

The salesperson rolled her eyes. Then she patiently explained to me how to tell the difference between the real and the fake when it came to high-end handbags.

Whether it's about dating or life in general, I like to believe that you can always learn something from every new experience. Something positive can always come out of something negative. In this case, I learned something I didn't know before about stitching and material on high-end bags. I was stunned that Walter thought I was that stupid. Did he and his wife really believe I wasn't going to be able to figure out the difference between a real and a fake Louis Vuitton?

Soon after my trip to the Miracle Mile, I confronted my boss's wife. I was quite angry and didn't pull any punches. At the time, she was carrying a real Hermès bag—which, I would like to add, my work had helped pay for.

"You both should be ashamed of yourself," I said. "I made you a great deal of money this year, and you can't even fulfill your promise to give me a bonus. At the very least, this should be a real Louis Vuitton. But instead you gave me a fake!"

She seemed embarrassed and told me that, indeed, it had fallen off a truck, but she excused herself by saying that she had thought it was real. That was the final straw.

I hated leaving Mark and my friends behind, but it was time for me to look for another job. I ended up with the same kind of sales job, but a different boss. His name was Seth. He was a younger guy, with a background in the financial industry. Seth, who wanted to break into a new field, had heard about my sales experience; he asked me to help him build his business and offered me a vice president position. I immediately hired a group of salespeople I had worked with before, creating a very strong team.

When I went to work for Seth, I was more interested in my commission and override than I was in my salary. Strong salespeople know that if you are good at what you do, that's how you make more money. Seth started out with four salespeople working in a modest fifteen-hundred-square-foot office. By the time I left, he had sixty-eight salespeople, and we were working in a huge office in a good building. Nobody could deny that I was instrumental in building his business.

It also goes without saying that Walter (of the fake handbag) asked me to come back. But I said, "No way!" Working all these sales job showed me that few people are better than I am at sales. To be good at sales, you have to be good at psychology and have common sense. I like to think that all those psychology courses I took in college paid off. As a salesperson, I also pride myself on being honest and having integrity.

Working for Seth, I began to get even more experience in some of the problems women can face as part of the workforce. Some of the guys loved having a woman boss, but you could tell that others started out hating it. It took them a while to let go of an outdated attitude about working for women. More than once when I asked someone to do something, I heard the response, "Yes, boss lady," said with a certain level of sarcasm.

Most of the managers and people Seth did business with were men. At business meetings, I was usually the only woman in the room. For the most part, they grew to treat me as "one of the guys." Sometimes this was good; other times not so much. They had no difficulty, for example, in discussing their indiscretions in front of me. I began to get a better firsthand understanding about just how many men were cheating. Some of them had rules about their infidelity. They would only fool around, for example, when they were out of town. Listening to them talk could become uncomfortable, but I would remind myself that I was learning a great deal about men.

I remember a business meeting with guys from out of town who wanted to go to a topless bar. Well, I thought, this is going to be uncomfortable. But I did it. Most of the men were wearing business suits, so was I. The only other women in the bar were wearing next to nothing. *Why*, I asked myself, *would these men want to go to a topless bar to discuss business?* Then a little light bulb went off in my head. *They are guys. Just accept it.* I just went along with the program and watched as some of them dropped what was probably thousands of dollars tipping the dancers.

I ended up making a fair amount of money working for Seth. It allowed me to save money, buy a car, and take vacations. Susan and I went to London and Paris. Lorraine and I took a ten-day cruise in Italy, Turkey, and Greece. There were, however, a few drawbacks working for Seth. For one thing, my job was 24-7. Seth would call whenever he wanted to talk about something, and the phone would often ring at ten o'clock or later at night.

Soon after I started working for Seth, he began to encourage me to buy a house. I could almost see the little wheels turning in his head. It wasn't difficult to figure out that he had an ulterior motive: he wanted me to have a mortgage and more debt. With more debt, I would be less likely to leave the job. But thinking about my situation realistically, I had to acknowledge that Seth was probably right. I needed the equity a house would bring. After talking it over with friends and family, I decided that buying would be the right move.

I looked at houses in all parts of Long Island's North Shore. Ideally, I wanted a move-in-ready colonial in an area that was closer to the highways and NYC. I absolutely didn't want a high ranch. I also knew I didn't want to be in the Bayville area, which is where my parents lived, because it was primarily a family area with few singles. My mother kept trying to talk me into a condo so I would have fewer problems with upkeep, but I wanted my very own backyard.

After two years of walking in and out of houses with large "for sale" signs in their yards, I finally found what I thought would be the right house for me. It was everything I said I didn't want: a high ranch close to my parents in Bayville. It needed a ton of work, there were few, if any, other singles in the area, and I was a good distance from any of the highways.

When I first looked at the house, I walked out on the deck in back, which had a lovely view of a creek. I could imagine myself sitting there feeling serene, having a cup of coffee in the morning and looking at the water. The configuration of the house meant that, down the road, it would be possible, if necessary, for my parents to move in with me. The house was an easy walk to the public beach, and a seven-minute ride to my parents' house, which was right off the Bayville Beach.

I remember asking myself if I really wanted to go from an $800-a-month rental to a large mortgage, taxes, and the expense of house maintenance. It was a big jump for me, but I did it. I signed on the dotted line for my mortgage, saying, "God help me!"—and He did. So there I was with a new house and no husband, or even a boyfriend, in sight.

Just about everything in the house needed work. The first thing I did was put in central air. There was no way I could live without serious air conditioning. My hair was too curly and frizzy! The kitchen and a bathroom needed to be completely replaced, and everything required painting and plastering. The floors needed redoing; ditto the driveway. I definitely have a shoe problem and consequently turned one of the smaller bedrooms into a walk-in closet.

I couldn't have done all this work without my parents, who lived close enough to show up to supervise contractors while I was at work. My father, as always, was my rock. He could fix or make just about anything and proved it by making me new lounge chairs for my deck. I loved my finished house. It had light hardwood floors; the kitchen cabinets were vanilla bean, and the granite had a beautiful brown-blue sparkle. When I walked into the kitchen, it made me smile.

I would say that it was a great house to live in alone, but for much of the time that I lived there, I was not alone. My friend Steven came back to the East Coast, and he stayed with me for close to a year. As always, Steven was a complete pain as well as a great help when it came to shopping, fashion, cleaning, and getting dressed. I could talk to him about anything, and he always told it like it was, whether I wanted to hear it or not. Steven and I even did mud face-masks together and egg-and-mayonnaise hair treatments.

Nobody could ever make me laugh like Steven. I remember one hot summer night I had a date, and as I was almost ready to walk out the door, Steven announced, "You can't go out like that. This date could be Mr. Right, and you're going out with a muffin top!"

I'm a size two, but it's true, sometimes I have just little bit of belly fat. Steven told me to put on a pair of panty hose to hold it in. It was summer. Who wants to wear panty hose in the summer? But I did it.

"Not good enough," Steven said as he looked me over. "Put on another pair on top of this pair."

"Are you kidding me?" I asked. Nonetheless, I followed his instructions and started trying to put another pair over the first pair. But I couldn't pull them up.

Steven jumped in to help. Within minutes, I was flat on the bed, and Steven and I were both trying to push and pull the second pair of stockings over the first. I was laughing so hard, I cried. He was finally able to finish the job. When I walked out the door, I was literally sweating my butt off. But at least there was no more muffin top!

Shortly after Steven moved out, my brother got divorced; he then moved into the downstairs for close to two years. My brother is a gourmet cook, so I didn't complain.

Something else happened while I was in that house that I want to put out as a warning for all singles. I believe somebody tried to dope me with a date-rape drug. I was at an engagement party with my parents, and the only thing I had to drink was one champagne cocktail as a toast. There were a large group of people there I knew. One of them, a man I had worked with in the past, started to talk to me. I told him that I had come there in my parents' car and was just waiting for them to leave.

"If you want to go home," he said. "I'm about to leave. You are on my way, and I can give you a ride."

"Great," I replied.

On the way, he stopped to put gas in the car, which I thought was a little strange because the tank looked three-quarters full to me. He also went into the convenience store at the station. When he returned, he had two bottles of water, and he handed me one of them. I noticed that the cap had been loosened, but I assumed he had done that for me and didn't think much about it. By the time, we reached my house, which was about fifteen minutes away, I was feeling completely woozy, and my words were slurring. He acted as though that was completely normal and almost carried me out of the car into my house. I really didn't know what was going on, but luck was with me, because my brother was there. When he heard the door open, he came up the stairs. The guy dropped me in a chair and left. I have no memory of anything else for most of the next day.

When I finally woke up, I felt as though I had been doped. And I think I was. I tell this story just to remind other women to never, ever take an open container of anything to drink and also to never, ever leave a drink unguarded at a bar or restaurant. These things happen and are very much part of to-day's single scene. I had no proof of what I'm sure happened, and there was nothing I could do about it except make certain that I was never alone with the man.

Along about this time, I decided once again that I needed to change jobs. My deal with Seth had always been that I was working primarily on commission, but he suddenly decided that this should change. Instead, he wanted me to start working on a straight salary. It was a very good salary, to be honest, but as far as I was concerned, I would still be taking a cut in pay. I told him I wouldn't do it.

He reminded me, as I thought he might, that I had a mortgage and other expenses. He said, "Any woman would jump at this salary and the security of this job."

Maybe he was right, but I felt that he was reneging on our original deal. At that point, it probably had more to do with the principle than it did with the money. I told him I was leaving.

As I started thinking about looking for a new job, I called my friend Mark. We agreed to meet for coffee. At that meeting, we decided that maybe it was time for both of us to go out on our own. We formed a partnership, and we have been working together ever since.

Tonia's Tips:
Learn from My Experience
Staying Independent

A friend of mine tells me that soon after she moved into her own apartment, she sat in her living room staring at the boxes of books that had not been unpacked. She realized that she really needed to get some shelving up, so she went to her local hardware store and explained her problem to the manager.

"I need a man," she said.

"Honey, you don't need a man," he replied. "You need an electric drill."

Whether she is buying a house, starting a business, building a career, the typical woman needs to acknowledge her own independence and become less fearful of developing strong coping skills. Remember, if the Statue of Liberty can stand on her own, so can you!

Practical Tools and Skills for Independence

Every woman needs to own a basic tool kit. You don't need anything complicated, but you do need a screwdriver, pair of pliers, a couple of hammers, and, yes, an electric drill. Know how to use these things, so you are able to put up a shelf, hang a picture, or tighten a drawer.

You also need a flashlight, extra batteries, candles, matches, and a good insect repellant.

Be prepared to have at least a few rodents (and I don't mean love rats) cross your path. My friend Judy says that the first time she saw a mouse in her house, she climbed on the kitchen table and screamed. After about five minutes, she realized that there was nobody there to come to her aid. With that in mind, make certain you have contact information for a reliable exterminator.

Even if you live in an apartment, you need to know how to shut off the water, change a fuse, and have a basic understanding of how your electrical breakers work.

Wherever you live, don't forget to invest in strong locks, a good alarm system, including fire and burglar alarms, and—very important—carbon monoxide detectors.

If you decide to buy a house, there will be a great deal to learn. For example, you will need to know what to do so that your pipes don't freeze and burst in cold weather. I'm speaking from experience here. You will also need to have your burner/boiler checked once a year and fireplaces inspected regularly.

Any homeowner, male or female, should become familiar with what's going on at Home Depot, Lowe's, Ace, or your most convenient local hardware store. It also helps to develop your own list of reliable plumbers, electricians, and handypersons as well as people to take care of your outside property. Think lawns and snow removal.

Get a Handle on Your Financial Situation

My mother had nothing to do with managing our household finances. My father was in charge of paying bills and balancing the checkbook. When my dad got sick and passed, my mother had a lot of catching up to do.

In her generation, her situation was not unusual. Times, of course, have changed, but many women still resist becoming completely familiar with their financial situation. You should understand your taxes and have a good retirement plan. So, do whatever you need to do to get a handle on your finances. For some people, this means having a meeting with an accountant or a financial advisor. Don't assume that your finances will take care of themselves. And don't spend money you don't have!

Understand What Men Really Think about Independent Women

Some men love a successful woman who stands on her own two feet. Others are definitely intimidated and uncomfortable. Still others may try to take advantage of you. This is one of the things you need to evaluate about any man you seriously date.

If you own your own home, for example, whether it is a studio apartment in a large city or three thousand square feet of suburban or bucolic bliss, you are sending out a clear message that you are an independent women.

Realize that some men may be threatened by your independence and/or success. You want to have a successful career along with financial independence and stability, but you don't want your partner to feel minimized by this. You want the man in your life to embrace your success and support your triumphs, just as women have always done for men.

But realize not all men feel this way. Some guys jump to the conclusion that because you stand on your own, you don't need a man. Remember to let the man in your life know that you need him because you love him and cherish your emotional connection.

But how about the other kind of guy? I'm talking about the man who looks at an independent woman and wants to be taken care of, thinking "Mother!" or, worse, "Payday!" Be wary of the man who gets the wrong impression and assumes you have more money than you do, or the man who expects you to pay for more than your share. You have to ask yourself if he is with you for love or for what he perceives to be your deep pockets.

Many women who own their own homes tell stories about men who are strongly attracted to the setup where they can move in, get a home-cooked meal, put their feet up on the couch, and take charge of the remote control.

Protect Your Space

If you own your own home, often other people may want to stay with you for a period of time. My brother stayed with me for more than a year, which was great because he's a fabulous cook who also cleans. Steven also stayed with me. This was great because he is a lot of fun. He doesn't cook, but he's an expert at ordering in and eating out. But people you may not love and appreciate can also invite themselves into your life, and I'm not just talking about men. Think twice before being so openhearted and kind that you end up with your local Single White Female camped out in the spare room.

9

Engaged!

It was a few days before Christmas, and I was coming down with something unhealthy. It felt like a killer cold. My throat was beginning to hurt; my nose was stuffed; all I wanted to do was go home and get into bed. But that wasn't going to happen. It was the holiday season—the time to be festive and exhausted. I had just worked a full day, and now I still had presents to buy and wrap. I had also promised Heather, a friend at work, that we could go out for a quick drink, but I didn't want to do it. When I told her that I needed to cancel, she had other ideas and seemed determined to get me to change my mind.

"Food will make you feel better," Heather said. "Let's go out. You can have a burger. You'll feel energized after you eat something. You need protein."

In my dazed state, I thought maybe she was right. Maybe food would fix my problem. The protein argument won out. We headed for a local steak house and sat at the bar. That's how I met Vinnie. The first time I saw him, his Mediterranean blue eyes and wavy dark hair hit me like an immediate concussion.

He had that movie-star aura like a young Mel Gibson or John Stamos. I admit it: it was a look that melted my brain faster than a hot knife cutting through butter. Or maybe my brain was melting because I was running a fever.

Vinnie walked into the bar with a friend, and I could immediately see other women staring at him, but he came over and starting talking to me. His friend focused on Heather.

What did we talk about? Well, I told him that I had bought a house and was renovating my kitchen. He told me that he was renting a condo and that he didn't think buying real estate at that time would be a wise investment.

He told me that he liked his work but explained that his real passion was golf. He said that golf came before anything else. The part about golf being his first love and coming before anything else didn't really sink in. This was clearly one of those times when I wasn't paying enough attention to what I was being told.

"Oh," I said. "My parents play golf, and I've taken a few lessons."

"I'll teach you," he said.

We exchanged other information. It turned out that he was also Italian American. He also grew up on Long Island. He also liked the beach.

What else did I need to know? On paper, we were a good match. Or were we?

The truth is that as good looking as he was, and despite the similarities in our backgrounds, I didn't think he was right for me. Or maybe I didn't think I was right for him. Just one of those gut reactions that I again chose to ignore. When he asked for my phone number, I gave it to him. I didn't really want to go out with him, but I also didn't want to lie to him or be impolite. In my head I thought, if he calls me, which I didn't think he would, I'd deal with it then.

Vinnie obviously sensed that I wasn't really responding to him, because he asked Heather, "Is this Tonia's real number?"

Heather looked at me. I nodded yes, and she looked at Vinnie and confirmed the number.

Vinnie called right away, but I had valid excuses for not making a date. It was Christmas; I had family plans; and then, of course, there was that sore throat and stuffed nose, which had turned into a full-blown case of the flu.

Vinnie called me on New Year's Eve. I was home in bed, still coughing. He was also home. We were both watching the same movie on television *The Holiday*, with Cameron Diaz. We stayed on the phone for hours talking about our lives and about the movie. Remember that split-screen scene in *When Harry Met Sally*, with Sally and Harry watching the same movie from their separate beds while talking on the phone? That's how it was.

Finally, Vinnie said, "Well, are we going to go out or not?"

We were having fun talking, and I had run out of excuses. For our first date, we returned to the steak house where we met, and we had drinks. Then we had dinner. Before I knew it, we were seeing each other several times a week. Those blue eyes turned out to be stronger than any concerns I might have felt about whether we were right for each other. I discovered that, like me, he was a Catholic. He didn't go to church regularly like I did, but he agreed to go with me. Okay, so he was less than enthusiastic about church attendance, but I never asked for perfection.

There was a lot for a woman to like about Vinnie besides those blue eyes. He could be very romantic and attentive. Every time I went to his apartment, he had candles lit and soft music playing. He also always had a glass of wine poured for me. In some ways, his attitude was metrosexual, which I liked. He was definitely into taking care of his appearance and buying the best hair and skin products. He meditated and did yoga, and often when I walked into his apartment after work, I would find him hanging upside down on an inversion table.

I liked that Vinnie was good-natured about going to the mall and shopping with me. I had recently dated a couple of men who were picky eaters, so I appreciated that Vinnie loved food. Even more important, he was always enthusiastic about my cooking.

I think I should also mention here that one of the best things about Vinnie was his family. I loved them. His mother was very sweet and kind. The first holiday I spent with them was on Easter; we had been dating more than four months, and we went to their home for a wonderful dinner. It felt very comfortable and familiar. They lived in a cute house on Long Island. His mother reminded me of my mother, my sister, and me. We were raised to try to please others and put others' needs first; she was the same way. She bustled around making sure that there was enough food on the table and that everybody was comfortable and accommodated. His father was very nice, and I immediately felt as though his sister was a friend. I'm very traditional, so of course I baked a cake to bring with me, along with some other pastry from a good Italian bakery, and I think they appreciated the gifts. I hate it when people come for dinner and don't sincerely offer to help, so I made a point of getting up to clean off the table and help with dishes as well as the pots and pans. And, of course, I wanted them to like me.

Vinnie lived ten minutes from the business I had only recently opened. Sometimes he just dropped in to say hello. Once he bought me a tree, which looked good next to my office window; another time he helped me hang pictures. I appreciated that he was supportive about my work and that I could talk to him about day-to-day problems.

I should also say that we didn't always spend that much time together. Vinnie was often busy, playing golf or doing his own things, but, at that time, that sort of fit into my schedule. I was also working long hours at my new business. I think women with busy careers sometimes don't notice if their husbands or boyfriends are not always available to do things. They may even feel a little bit grateful, because fewer demands are being made on them. For me, that was definitely the case.

Vinnie and I had known each other less than six months when we began to talk about marriage. The first time it happened, we were having dinner at the steak house where we originally met.

Vinnie looked at me and said, "I love you, and I want to spend the rest of my life with you. I can see us spending the rest of our lives together."

I said, "I love you too."

He said, "Let's go look for ring settings together."

So we did. At that moment, we were both on the same page.

We even agreed about which local jewelry store to visit, and within days, we had chosen an amazing ring. That was in June, but the formal proposal didn't come until July. After dinner at a lovely restaurant facing the water, we took a walk on Bayville Beach, which faces Long Island Sound. It was a beautiful sunset; you could see the boats gently bobbing on the calm water and the lights just beginning to come on across the sound in Connecticut.

On this perfect summer evening, Vinnie suggested that we climb up on the lifeguard stand to watch the remains of the sunset. When we got to the top and sat down, he pulled a ring box out of his pocket and handed it to me. It was a very matter-of-fact gesture. He could have been handing me a bagel with cream cheese. At that exact second, there was a gust of wind, and a dark cloud rolled over our heads. Some people say rain is good luck, but this was just a dark cloud and wind. The weather had changed so suddenly. I looked up at the sky as we started running for the car. It was an extremely dark and ominous cloud, and I couldn't help but wonder if we were already falling into a downward spin.

We went straight to my parents' house. Vinnie had told them what to expect, and they had a bottle of champagne ready. We showed them the ring, and we called his parents to share the news. As I stood there with a champagne glass in my hand, I remember looking at the ring and thinking, *This is a beautiful ring, but is this the right person?*

One of the people we called to share the news was my friend Madeleine. I trusted Madeleine, and her approval was almost as important to me as my parents' approval. I could hear the hesitation in her voice. "Tonia," she said, "I hope you will be happy. But are you sure you're not rushing into this? Take your time. Get to know him a little better."

Madeleine's question stayed with me. Was I simply following Vinnie's lead and rushing into this engagement without giving it enough thought? Was I settling?

Blame It on the Raccoons

Let's talk about what was going in my mind at the time. I was turning thirty-nine. That's a big number for women who want to get married. And, more than anything else, I wanted children. In terms of my business, every day I faced new problems. I loved that I was no longer working for another person, but having a new business meant that there was a fair amount of stress. Then there was the house I had recently bought and was in the process of renovating on my own. Sure, it was wonderful, and I was proud of my strength and independence, but there were definitely times that I wished I had a partner to help me make decisions—preferably one who knew more about plumbing than I did. And then there were the raccoons!

The raccoons may be one of the scariest things that ever happened to me. There were so many of them! They invaded my yard, and they threatened to invade my house. They would come at night, circle the house, and rattle the doors. I remember one night, looking out the window and seeing their beady little eyes. I started to scream. About thirty seconds into my scream, I realized nobody could hear me but the raccoons. There was nobody to come to my aid. You can't call the police about raccoons, and I didn't want to bother my father again. I have a lot of shoes, so I started throwing shoes at the raccoons to make them go away. As I did this, I remember praying to God, saying, "Please say this is a cruel joke. Please send me a man!"

I can deal with a lot, but not being invaded by raccoons. I had also heard that some raccoons carry rabies, so that added to my anxiety. Okay, I wasn't out there playing with them, but I'd be out there in the morning cleaning up the garbage pails that they had ransacked.

Of course I did what any reasonable person would do under these circumstances; I called the raccoon guy to come, trap them, and take them someplace more rural where they would be happy and leave me alone. This introduced a whole new problem: the raccoon guy. He was so sleazy. He just kept looking at me with his attempt at seductive eyes and asking me if I was married and where my husband was. Weird! What business was it of his to ask about my marital status and my husband? Naturally, I told him that I was married but that my husband was working late. There were a lot of raccoons, and the guy had to return many times. Each time, we would go through the same routine. "Where is your husband now?" the guy would ask. On each visit, he got scarier and scarier looking. Once I did ask my father to come over while he was there, and I seriously considered asking my good neighbor, Mike, to come over and pretend to be my husband.

Between the raccoons and the raccoon guy, I began to feel more and more that nobody needed this much independence. I've talked to other single women about this, and most of them have told me that it is common to sometimes feel as though it is all too much.

At those times, many women long for a 1950s *Leave It to Beaver* life. They want to know what it feels like to be June Cleaver, with her little pearls, being taken care of by Ward, who handles all the big decisions and big problems, not to mention pays all the bills. I know that, at this point in my life, there is no way that I would want to live this kind of life. But for just a moment back there, when raccoons were surrounding my house, that's what I wanted. I also knew that Vinnie wasn't really that kind of man. But at least he would be there to help me deal with the raccoons, and I wouldn't have to be afraid of the pest control guy getting ideas.

I was positive that the time had come to get married!

Tonia's Tips:
Learn from My Experience
Find Out What He Is Really Like

Many women have told me that they remember important things they were told in the beginning of their relationships, which they foolishly ignored at the time. Later, looking back, they realized that they'd been given strong clues to where potential problems might be hiding. When I first started dating, I know I did not pay enough attention to what my dates said. Big mistake! I guess I had a case of selective hearing. On your first few dates with someone, you can tell a great deal about what he is going to be like as a long-term romantic partner by what he emphasizes in his own life.

- The first thing to check out is whether he is kind and compassionate. Ask about his family, kids (if he has them), nieces/nephews, dog, cat, or iguana. Pay attention to everything he says. How he talks about those closest to him will tell an important story. If your date says, "I hate my mother or my sister," don't be surprised if he isn't strong on the importance of family. If he tells you about how he was dishonest in his financial dealings with his ex, don't expect that to change with you. If he says, "All pets should be microwaved," don't anticipate that he will feed your bird, walk your dog, or snuggle up with your cat.

- Notice his behavior. How does he act toward the waitperson? If he is curt and unkind, this attitude may prevail in the rest of his life, and you probably won't be able to count on him to gently place an icepack on your head if you have a migraine. On the other hand, if he flirts with the waitress or hostess, you might want to prepare yourself for a lifetime of watching him pay excessive attention to other women. And yes, once again, if he carefully splits the bill in half and tells you that you owe $21.32 for your glass of wine and portion of the shared crab cake appetizer, you probably shouldn't anticipate lovely gifts or a future with a generous man.

- What does he talk about? What's important to him? If he is fixated on subjects that don't interest you in the slightest, this is something you should know. Does he talk too much about himself? Does he have a spiel about his life that seems almost prepared? Does he have too many overly dramatic stories about other women, including his exes? If he tells you how much his ex hates him or has too many anecdotes of what she did to hurt him, you may need to wonder about her reasons why. When you ask him questions, does he seem to be withholding information? Most important: Does he ask you questions about yourself? And is he genuinely interested in your answers?

- Observe how your date acts under routine circumstances, because under stress his behavior will likely be exaggerated. Angry men can become angrier and even violent. Grumpy men become even grumpier. Drinkers will drink more. Liars will become even better liars.
- Notice any extreme behavior. If he's overly intense, overly talkative, overly boring, or even overly interested in you, it's worth paying attention to.

The rule: don't tolerate or make excuses for extreme conduct just because he's attractive, successful, or charming. In fact, if he is too charming, remind yourself that his dating style may be based less on sincerity than it is on well-practiced sales techniques.

Find Out If You Agree on the Big Issues

Perhaps neither one of you cares that much about politics. But if one of you is a determined progressive while the other stands firmly in the conservative camp, it's unlikely that you're going to have an easy time of it. The same kind of thing is true with religion. If one of you goes to church on a regular basis and the other is a complete nonbeliever, you need to know this early on. If neither of you is a church member but you both think of yourselves as spiritual beings, you have a shared attitude. But what happens if one of you has spiritual interests, and the other makes fun of these interests and thinks they are silly? This could certainly spell trouble. Early dates will help you figure out whether you are on the same page about those things that are important to you. It takes a long time to get a true sense of what somebody is like, but you can certainly get an idea of areas where you might have disagreements.

Find Out More about Him

The sooner you get to meet his family, the better. Knowing them will tell you so much more about him. You also want to find out how he lives. Take a good look at his home. Is he overly messy or sloppy? Can you live with someone who is surrounded by so much clutter? Or is he fastidious and neat to the point where it borders on compulsive behavior?

You also want to know if his sense of humor matches yours. Do you find the same things funny? Can you laugh at things together, or is he too serious to crack a smile or a joke?

Does he tend to be controlling? Many women complain about partners who insist upon controlling everything from the thermostat to the contents in the refrigerator. Minor control issues can be worked out in a relationship, but, let's face it, some women are very unhappy because they live with men who want to control everything they do. Controlling men are sometimes extremely jealous. At the beginning of a relationship, it can feel flattering to be with a man who is jealous when anyone else pays attention to you. Later on, these jealousy issues can turn into a nightmare.

What about sex? Is something about his behavior telling you up front that he has some preferences that you think are strange, weird, or just downright icky? If he tells you, for example, that he and his ex watched *Fifty Shades of Grey* every night, and that isn't your style, don't say you weren't forewarned. A friend of mine was horrified when a man she almost married told her that he and his best friend left work early in order to have a threesome. She couldn't go through with the marriage because this story haunted her. In this modern world, hard-core porn is also an issue of disagreement in many relationships. If he is a porn addict, and just the idea of porn drives you up a wall, as a couple you are probably not destined for romantic bliss.

And let's not forget about his basic attitude toward money. Does he believe in being frugal? Is he generous? When it comes to money, is he fair and honest? Does he try to take advantage of you? Don't ignore potential problems because you think it's not all that big a deal. In fact, not being on the same page as far as money is concerned is frequently a contributing factor in breakups.

In the beginning of a relationship, it's human to focus on the good in a man, particularly when you are physically attracted to him. We practice selective noticing. Be aware of this, and be cautious.

Finally, Beware of the Man Who Seems Too Good to Be True

Realize that many men tell you what you want to hear just to get you, pretending to be people they are not. Some of these men may just want to get you into the sack for the night; others see a good catch and want you long term. Many women realize long after they have said "I do" that they had been told things that weren't true. Long term, this doesn't work out well for either party.

10

Not So Fast!

I first saw the gown in a bridal magazine, where it looked exactly like the gown I always wanted. After several phone calls, I managed to track it down to a store on Long Island not far from where I lived. The time had finally come for me to go shopping for a traditional bridal gown for what was planned to be a very traditional wedding. As expected, my mother came with me. I also asked my father, because he had terrific taste, was always impeccably dressed, and he would be walking me down aisle. And, of course, how could I go shopping without Steven? I knew I would end up feeling grateful for his brutal honesty, with an emphasis on brutal.

I tried on several dresses, but everybody agreed that my original choice, which was an exquisite shade of white with just a touch of cream, was gorgeous. My mother worried about the alterations, and my always reliably honest friend Steven told me I needed to lose a few pounds, something I expected from him no matter what I weighed. My father didn't say much, but when I looked at him, I could see a little bit of moisture in his blue eyes. His youngest daughter was finally getting married! My father, who never cried, looked as though he wanted to.

Soon, there was a repeat visit to the shop with my sister, Jolene, who was going to be my matron of honor. Vinnie's sister and my friend Lorraine, my bridesmaids, were also there as well as my niece, Alexa, who was looking forward to being a junior bridesmaid. Because we were planning a fall wedding, we chose gowns in a beautiful, rich chocolate brown.

We were very fortunate, because the venue we were interested in had a cancellation, and they were able to give us a Sunday in October. The date was set, and invitations went out. But there was still so much to do. We had to visit caterers and bakers and florists. We had to taste appetizers and entrees and cake, lots of cake. So many decisions, so little time!

We were going to be married in the Catholic church that I attended. Although Vinnie was also Catholic, he wasn't a regular churchgoer. That bothered me, but I managed to overlook it. Because we were going to be married by a priest in a church, we were expected to take part in what is known as a Pre-Cana course. In our case, this course was a daylong seminar given for a group of couples on a Saturday. In Pre-Cana, couples come together to discuss a variety of subjects that will almost inevitably come up in the course of a marriage. These include everything from how to make financial decisions to attitudes on housework, intimacy, and children.

When we arrived at the course, we were all given long questionnaires to fill out. The answers to these questions reflected our individual attitudes. When Vinnie and I exchanged our answers, it was immediately apparent that we disagreed on many essential subjects. I was shocked. Did we really know so little about each other? We weren't the only couple facing challenges that Saturday. We were still struggling through our answers when we noticed another couple, who were raising their voices. Another man in our group actually walked out, followed soon after by his fiancée. They did both return, but it was obvious that things were becoming very tense.

After the Pre-Cana session was finished, all the couples were encouraged to attend mass together. I thought it would make us closer; I wanted the experience of praying with Vinnie and holding his hand. But Vinnie didn't want to do it. I could see from his expression that he just wanted to get out of there as quickly as possible. I found this very upsetting. Later, he and I got into a huge argument in the car on the way home. We both worked at smoothing it over, but still, it was starting to become apparent that there were things we needed to discuss further.

As we got closer to our wedding date, it turned out that there were other problems. I had been having some pains in my side, and I decided to visit my gynecologist to be sure that there was nothing strange going on with my ovaries. Vinnie and I had talked about having children, and I hoped to get pregnant soon after we got married. It was important to be sure that I had a clean bill of health.

After visiting the doctor, I discovered that there was something wrong, and it had nothing to do with my ovaries. Because he wasn't sure where my pain originated, the doctor ordered some scans, one of which showed that I had what appeared to be an aneurysm on my spleen. The doctor explained that this condition was very rare—and affected only 1 percent of the population.

"Have you ever been in an accident?" he asked. "This could be the result of an accident or some sort of trauma."

Years earlier, I had been in an accident, but I didn't remember having any pain. Whatever the reason, there was only one solution: surgery. The doctor was positive that if I didn't have the surgery and then became pregnant, I would run a high risk of dying from a ruptured aneurysm. Deciding what to do was a no-brainer.

The doctors were also unsure about how extensive the surgery would be. If I was fortunate, it would be a simple procedure with a short recovery time, but there was a fifty-fifty chance that I would need more complicated surgery with at least a six-week recovery time. I remember asking my mother to please not tell relatives and friends what was wrong. I was so upset that I didn't want to talk about it. And I certainly didn't want any phone calls from people who were feeling sorry for me.

Nonetheless, it seemed as though the most reasonable thing to do was to postpone the wedding. We were able to convince the venue to change the date, and we sent out notices to everyone we had invited, telling them that the wedding was postponed, without giving them a reason. The wedding was rescheduled for May. I worried a little about what people would think, but I had more important things to think about.

The Pre-Cana had opened my eyes to the possibility that Vinnie and I would have to do some work if we were going to learn to compromise about our differences. But in the meantime, there were other issues that I certainly didn't anticipate.

One of our first problems presented itself on Halloween. Now, let me start out by saying that I am phobic about clowns. I know that this is not your average run-of-the-mill phobia, but I'm not alone in feeling this way. There is even a name for the phobia; it's called coulrophobia. Whatever it's called, the fact remains that clowns terrify me. Really terrify me! It all started when my mother took me to my pediatrician as a toddler. I remember walking in the waiting room and seeing pictures of clowns. One particular picture scared the life out of me, and I started crying. Thinking about it even today upsets me. As was to be expected, I associated clowns with visits to the doctor. Of course I had told Vinnie about this in the early days of our relationship when we were sharing information about each other. Vinnie and I had a plan to go out to dinner that Halloween night; Steven would be joining us.

I was home giving out little packets of candy to the neighborhood trick-or-treaters when Vinnie called to say he was going to be late meeting us at the restaurant. I called Steven to let him know. Just as I hung up, there was a loud banging on my door. I looked out, expecting more trick-or-treaters, but instead, it was a large, obviously adult clown—think Clarabell—who was banging on my door, ringing the buzzer, and jiggling the doorknob. I do understand that my fear of clowns is a little bit strange and over the top, but I can't control my reactions.

I went into full panic-attack mode. I also understood that I couldn't call the police on Halloween and say, "Please do something! There's a clown at my door!" So I called my father. In the meantime, my next-door neighbor noticed this large clown banging on my door and started to come over. Looking out my window, I could see him crossing my lawn, which immediately relaxed me enough so that I could take a closer look at this terrifying clown. *It was Vinnie!*

I opened the door and played along. "Hello, Mr. Clown. Would you like some M&Ms?"

But I was furious. When you are about to marry someone, you want to believe that you can trust this person not to go out of his way to scare you. I didn't understand why Vinnie would do this. In the meantime, he thought it was absolutely hysterical. He could see from my still-shaking hands that I had been very frightened. Why would he think this was funny?

Later, in the restaurant, Vinnie went to the men's room, and I told Steven what had happened. He was genuinely taken aback. "Not even I would do that," Steven said.

And it turned out that Vinnie had at least one phobia of his own, which was going to impact our relationship. When Vinnie and I discussed where we were going to live after we were married, we had agreed that my house was the most practical solution. Remember, Vinnie didn't want to buy any real estate, and he lived in a one-bedroom apartment. My house was sitting there, waiting to be filled. But there was a problem. My house was a high ranch, and Vinnie was phobic about high ranches. I know how weird that sounds. Trust me, I also thought it was weird, and I certainly remember the expression on my mother's face when I told her about Vinnie's problems with my house. But it seems that Vinnie had an uncle of whom he was very fond. This uncle lived in a high ranch. This uncle also died in his high ranch house. And Vinnie, then in his twenties, was the one who discovered his uncle's body. End result: he wasn't sure that he would ever want to live in a high ranch.

While we were sorting out our issues with clowns and high ranches, the time came for me to have my surgery, which was done in a hospital in Manhattan on the Wednesday before Thanksgiving. I was very busy at work and had chosen this time so I would be taking fewer days off. Fortunately, my surgery was not that complicated, and my recovery time was relatively short. Vinnie and my mother had taken me to the hospital, and he stayed there with her while the operation was taking place.

I know he was trying his best to be supportive and loving, but spending time in a hospital room thinking about life-and-death issues gives you a sense of perspective about what matters in life. As I thought about everything that was going on, I realized that I was starting to feel more than a little nervous about our relationship.

By Christmas, I was recovered from the surgery. Vinnie spent Christmas Eve with his parents and then came over to my parents' for dessert. Christmas Day we reversed the procedure, and I went to Vinnie's parents' for dessert. But as time progressed, and our planned wedding day grew closer and closer, I was less and less sure about what I wanted to do. We were very different people. I'm a very outgoing and social person. Vinnie rarely wanted to spend time with friends, and when we did, he was very quiet, distant, and even withdrawn.

We took my niece and nephew out for Chinese food one night so that they could all get to spend some time together. They were shy and quiet, which is not how they normally are. Afterward, they both told me independently that they were a little afraid of Vinnie. My friend Madeleine, who was always supportive, kept asking me if I was sure I wanted to marry Vinnie. I trusted Madeleine, and I could tell that she had some reservations. We went out to dinner with another couple, also friends of mine, one evening, and afterward, the husband, who had known me for many years, said, "I don't know, Tonia. I would never have imagined that you would end up with somebody like Vinnie."

"What do you mean?" I asked him.

"You're so outgoing, and he's so reserved. I get the feeling he doesn't really want to be out with other people."

It was strange that my friend said that. His words rang true, though, because as time went on, I was getting the impression that I was one of the people Vinnie didn't want to spend time with. There were times when he almost appeared to be avoiding me. We would go out for dinner, and I would assume that he would return to my house, where we would hang out and watch television. But instead, he would drop me off and go home. This seemed like bizarre behavior. I wanted a husband who would be my best friend and do things with me. I wanted to feel a sense of sharing and closeness. Vinnie appeared to want the exact opposite. He wanted to know that he had a relationship with me, but he didn't seem to want to do anything that would bring us closer together.

I'm ashamed to admit this, but one night when Vinnie left early saying he was tired and wanted to go home, I jumped into my car and followed him. He headed for the steak house where we had met. Because I was actually wondering if he was meeting someone else, I waited ten minutes and then I went right in after him. He was sitting at the bar, having a drink, and obviously flirting with the female bartender. When I sat down next to him, he was annoyed and angry.

"What are you doing here?" I asked. "I thought you were going home."

"So I stopped for a drink," he replied. "What's the big deal?"

He was right. What was the big deal? He certainly didn't have to report in to me about every second of his life. But I didn't understand. What was going through his head that made him think he needed to hide things? His attitude was making me question whether we belonged together.

There was one other thing that bothered me: Vinnie was very quiet, and sometimes when we were with other people, I couldn't tell if he was staring into space or if he was staring at other women. I understand that men like to look at women, but his behavior was giving me pause. One weekend he went to Florida to play golf, and he didn't suggest that I go with him, which I found disturbing. That Saturday night, when I was wondering where he was and what he was doing, my phone rang. It was a friend of mine who, coincidently, was also in Miami.

"Guess where I am?" she asked.

"Where?"

"In Miami," she answered. "Are you down here?"

"No, I'm home."

"I'm asking," she told me, "because I'm outside a Hooters. And guess who I just saw going in?"

It wasn't a difficult guess. "Vinnie," I replied. "He's down there playing golf for the weekend, so he's probably meeting some of the guys."

"Guys will be guys," she said.

"Right," I answered. Vinnie going into Hooters told me that I didn't have to worry about his having a date with anybody else. But I knew Vinnie, and the chances were that he was not going into Hooters to meet some other guys. He was going alone.

I called Vinnie. "Hi," I said. I could hear bar noises in the background. "Where are you?"

"Oh," he answered, "I'm in the hotel lobby. Just heading up to my room."

I didn't call him on what I knew, because I didn't want him to feel as though I was spying on him. But that deeply disturbed me. I'm not the kind of woman who gets upset because her fiancé is hanging out in a Hooters. I am the kind of woman who gets upset when her fiancé lies to her. Why was he lying? It was another way of putting distance between us. His behavior was telling me that he had a whole life going on inside his head about which I knew nothing. When Vinnie wasn't with me, I was beginning to feel as though I needed to hire a private detective. What was that? I never could say for sure where he was, and I certainly didn't know what he was thinking. I didn't like this feeling, and I knew I didn't want to live with it for the rest of my life.

I looked at the beautiful diamond on my ring finger. One minute I was planning and looking forward to the perfect wedding; the next I knew I had to make a decision. Having a great marriage was more important to me than having the perfect wedding.

The first person I talked to about the possibility of canceling the wedding was our family priest, who had met Vinnie and was supposed to be officiating at the wedding. I told him that I had reservations, and I wasn't 100 percent sure whether I wanted to get married.

He was very supportive. "Lots of people get cold feet," he told me. "That's normal. You have to decide whether you are just feeling a little scared at the magnitude of what you are doing or if your reservations are real. If you end up deciding you don't want to go through with this, remember that it's better to make this decision now instead of later. It's not fair to either you or Vinnie to go forward with something that you don't really believe is going to work."

My brain was churning, and I didn't know what to do. I didn't want to hurt Vinnie. I certainly didn't want to hurt his family, particularly his sweet, sweet mother, who I knew had already purchased a beautiful and expensive dress.

That Sunday after mass, which I attended alone because Vinnie played golf on Sundays, I stopped at my parents' house. My brother and sister were also there. As he often did, my brother had brought the typical Sunday antipasto—sausage, roasted peppers, fresh mozzarella. I sat down with them.

"What's wrong?" my father asked.

"Yeah," my brother echoed.

"Are you okay?" my sister chimed in.

My mother just shook her head and stared at me.

"What makes you think something's wrong?" I asked.

"You're not eating." My mother said it first.

I told them what was on my mind and that I was thinking of canceling the wedding. I was worried about what everyone would think.

My family's words were almost identical to those of the priest. My father asked me if I was sure that I wasn't just having an ordinary case of cold feet. They all reminded me that marrying Vinnie if I was not 100 percent sure wouldn't be fair to either one of us.

The wedding was a month away.

That night when I spoke to Vinnie, I suggested we go away to Florida the following weekend. We had been fighting about so many things, and I told him that I thought our relationship needed work and we should spend some quality time together doing things, relaxing, and hanging out by the pool. I figured maybe if we were alone together, we could get closer. He agreed.

The following weekend, we headed off to Florida for a three-day vacation. As always, Vinnie brought his golf clubs. We were there for three days. For two of them, Vinnie played golf from sunup till sundown. The third day he spent with me, but I could see his heart wasn't in it. He really wanted to be on the golf course. When we got back to Long Island, he dropped me off at my house and left. There was no way I could avoid what was going on between us: whenever I tried to get closer, he moved further away. We wanted different things from a marriage.

A day later, I sat down with him and told him we needed to cancel the wedding. He offered some feeble resistance, but it wasn't enough. I took his beautiful ring off my finger and handed it back to him.

"No," he insisted. "You keep it."

When he said that, he showed me the generous, kind spirit that had made me fall in love with him.

"No," I told him as I handed the ring back to him. "It's not fair, and it wouldn't be right. The ring is yours."

The hardest part was going to be telling his parents.

Tonia's Tips:
Learn from My Experience
Does It Really Matter What Anybody Else Thinks?

Anybody who has ever taken a yoga or Pilates class is familiar with the term "strengthening your core." When the instructor tells you that one exercise or another will help strengthen your core, she is referring to all those muscles in the center of your body that make it possible for you to physically move with strength and confidence. But your physical core isn't the only part of you that needs to remain strong. If a woman is going to survive the dating world, she needs to be certain that she also has a strong and dependable emotional core, one she can rely on when she makes those important relationship decisions that may affect the rest of her life.

Too many of the dating decisions we make are influenced by what other people think. Almost as soon as we know that we like the little boy sitting next to us in second or third grade, we realize that other people are making judgments about our choices. It could be your best friend saying, "You like him? He has such thick glasses!" It could also be your parents saying, "Why don't you play with the little boy from across the street? We think he would be a better playmate." From that moment on, when you look at that little boy, all you can see are his glasses; all you can hear are your parents' voices questioning your judgment.

Other people might also say something about that little boy that influences your opinion.

The fact is that when it comes to figuring out exactly which potential romantic partners we find attractive, we are subjected to a great many outside influences, ranging from friends and family to media representations of how desirable a potential partner should look and act.

In short, the outside world plays a huge role in influencing our romantic decision making. We are trained from an early age to pay close attention to what others think. Yes, it's true that people often give us good advice, which is worth following. But there are moments when we spend so much time thinking about what other people are saying that we fail to listen to our reliable inner core.

I know firsthand that getting someone else's opinion on whether you should start or end a relationship can be reassuring. But—and this is a big *but*—nobody else will be living your life. In the long run, what someone else thinks or says shouldn't be the deciding factor. Another person's opinion may help you arrive at your own conclusions, but keep it in perspective. You need to have enough confidence in yourself so that you can make your own decision.

We have all had the experience of looking back and wondering, *Why didn't I listen to so-and-so?* or we can look back and wonder, *Why did I listen to so-and-so?* Our decisions are our own. Only you know the core you. Deep down, only you know what you want. Find the inner voice that is coming from your core, and follow it. Don't look back. Only look forward.

I know in my life, when each of my relationships ended—and I've had a few serious ones—I had to get over my sense of embarrassment, knowing that friends and family were comparing notes about how I'd let another one bite the dust, despite the fact that they didn't know the entire story. Sometimes ending relationships requires a strong sense of self, and you don't really want to share all the details of why this relationship wasn't good for you.

What matters is what *you* think about the choices you make. Yes, we all make mistakes, and we have to live with them, but what somebody else thinks should not be your biggest concern. You have to stay true to yourself. If someone thinks your date is too short, too tall, too old, too young, or too bald, recognize that you don't know that much about that person's partner or what goes on behind their closed doors. Maybe to the outside world, he is good looking and rich, but at home he's mean and smelly. Personally, I'd rather have the short, bald guy.

Remember, when we make decisions on our own, at least there is no one else to blame.

11

What Are My Options Now?

More than two hundred and fifty people had been invited to the wedding. With three weeks to go, everybody had to be uninvited; we had to send out all those cards telling would-be-guests that the wedding was canceled. My guilt was enormous. I thought about the more than eighty women who had come to my engagement party and given me gifts; I thought about all the people who had saved the date and had bought outfits to wear to the wedding, particularly Vinnie's mother, whose beautiful gown probably couldn't be returned. In fact, every time I thought about either of Vinnie's parents, I was overwhelmed with guilt.

Vinnie and I had split the cost of everything, and we had both lost thousands. I thought about all the money that we had put out for down payments on the venue, band, photographer, flowers, food, and printed invitations, not to mention the cake! I always admired Vinnie, because he didn't complain or make me feel even worse about the lost money. He made a good living, but he wasn't a gazillionaire. Nonetheless, when it came to money, Vinnie was a decent guy who always did the right thing. And, yes, of course I was guilty that I might have hurt him.

I was guilty about all of it. But I was also positive that not getting married was the right decision. I kept telling myself that the money we lost was small compared to what it would have cost if we had gone through with the wedding and ended up divorced. Even so, I was also guilty about my parents. Not only had I put them through the stress of planning a wedding, now I was putting them through the stress of having to speak to all those relatives who wanted to know exactly what happened. I, of course, called friends, who were all extremely supportive. Steven's response was entirely predictable: "Thank God you didn't end up with somebody who doesn't know how to dress!"

But my mother was getting the majority of the phone calls of the "So, is Tonia ever going to get married?" variety. As expected, all my aunts, uncles, and cousins were checking in with her.

Both of my parents were also worried about me. Going back to that first breakup with Ken, my mother and father had watched me recover from other relationships that ended. They knew that I would be depressed and sad. I might have been reluctant to marry Vinnie, but I loved him. I anticipated that ending our relationship meant that I would be feeling lonely and less than enthusiastic about life, and that's exactly what happened. It would be months before I would feel like dating again. During this time, I was very grateful that my family and friends were so supportive.

But there were other issues. Here I was, a forty-year-old woman! In the blink of an eye, I had gone from making plans for getting married and starting a family to wondering if I would always be alone. There was a white tan line on my left finger where my ring used to be. As I looked at that ring line, knowing how much I wanted a family, I couldn't help questioning my decision. Maybe I should have just gone through with the marriage so I could have had kids. However, as much as I wanted children, I knew that would have been the wrong thing to do.

When each of my serious relationships ended, I felt profound disappointment—not only because love ended, but also because I mourned the loss of the home and family that I had hoped for with this person. Each lost opportunity brought me to my knees with sadness. Now, I began to ask another question: okay, I didn't have a husband, but couldn't I still have children? Couldn't I do this—on my own? As I thought about it, I realized that I was a self-sufficient woman living in the twenty-first century. I had choices.

Like all those other women who approach their forties without a mate but who have not abandoned their dreams of motherhood, I began to consider my options. My friend Lorraine was in a similar stage of her life, so this became one of our regular topics of conversation. We would discuss getting pregnant and living near each other, or possibly even sharing the same house. I knew my mother and sister would help. We imagined our children as friends who would happily play together. We could share child-care expenses. We decided that my split-level ranch house would be ideal. We could each take a floor. Her parents also lived very close. How convenient would that be?

Lorraine and I were not alone. Millions of other women in our age group were faced with the same choices. We would have preferred the traditional route, but if the handsome prince doesn't show up as scheduled, the pressure to conceive grows and the window of opportunity narrows.

Although "single mother by design" doesn't carry the negative connotation that it did in past generations, I realized that having and raising a child alone was still a huge decision that carried a lifetime of responsibilities. Raising a child could bring great joy, but it would also present some awesome challenges. Most important, I had to be sure of what I was doing. Shopper that I am, I was completely aware that a pair of wickedly beautiful Christian Louboutin shoes with their signature lacquered red soles could be returned to Saks or Barneys if they hurt your feet, but children arrive without a return policy.

As I thought about having a child, I ran through my options for doing so: I could adopt, I could arrange for some form of sperm donorship, or I could have a child with a man I had no intention of marrying. But each of these options came with built-in issues.

Many people suggested that I try to adopt. "There are so many babies that need good homes!" was a sentence I heard many times. But I had to face the facts: it was highly unlikely that a healthy single woman who was giving her infant up for adoption would want to place it with another single woman. There are so many couples who desperately want to adopt babies; why would a birth mother choose me? I honestly didn't think that this could realistically happen. If I wanted to adopt, I would probably have to find an older child or a child from another country.

When I started researching this possibility, I began to read about the long list of problems that many well-intentioned couples have faced trying to provide good homes for children who were born with serious psychological issues caused by previous abuse or conditions like fetal alcohol syndrome. I didn't think I was a good candidate for sainthood, and I also didn't think I could handle this level of problem alone. There were so many unknowns in the adoption process. What would I do if everything went wrong?

How about getting pregnant on my own? Was that a possibility? I even had the weird thought of approaching one of several male friends and asking if I could borrow some sperm. But when I thought about this for longer than a minute, I could see all the potential problems. So could I choose the route of many other women: buy myself some sperm and see what happened? If the sperm is purchased through a sperm bank, certain rules apply. The donor will remain anonymous, and clients have no right to learn his identity or solicit identifying information. The donor has absolutely no responsibility to his biological offspring. Although genetic testing and disease-screening techniques are sophisticated and sensitive, they are not foolproof. The sperm bank cannot completely guarantee that the sperm provided will be free of disease or genetic abnormalities. Clients and donors are informed of their rights. The principle of informed consent is based on scientific and medical ethics. Translation: no laboratory can test the truthfulness of an individual.

Donors, whom you have to hope are being honest, submit specific personal information, including their physical description, hair color, height, ethnicity, and educational background. Clients are able to choose the sperm they want based on the donor's specific information. Since different clients often choose to select sperm from donors with similar traits, some sperm banks now limit the number of deposits a donor can make, thus limiting the number of offspring with the same father. This limit doesn't always exist. As strange as it might seem, half-brothers and half-sisters from the same donor father could wind up getting married and having children without knowing they were related. Now that's something to consider.

The major issue: I was over forty and might well have difficulty getting pregnant. This left me with the other venues to motherhood, specifically those that come under the general heading of assisted reproductive technology (ART). Yes, I'm talking about in vitro fertilization (IVF). Women today are encouraged to freeze their eggs while they are still in their twenties, but when I was in my twenties, I didn't even realize that this option existed. Women who freeze their eggs while they are still in their twenties and early thirties have a greater chance of getting pregnant. The fertility picture changes, however, if you wait until you are over the age of thirty-five to freeze your eggs. In my case, my biological clock was ticking very loudly, and my eggs were becoming even more mature.

If I were to take the first step, the IVF path would typically begin by my taking some form of prescribed fertility medication in order to stimulate egg production. The more eggs, the better! Eggs would then be retrieved from my ovaries using a small surgical procedure. The retrieved eggs would then be placed in a lab dish and exposed to purchased sperm, with the hope of creating several embryos that could then be placed inside my womb. Another method, intracytoplasmic sperm injection (ICSI), involves a single sperm injected directly into an egg. Both methods require a sperm donor, but there is certainly no sex, affection, or spontaneity. If the tick-tock of your biological clock is pressuring you to get the job done, and there's no appropriate guy on the horizon, this is a viable choice, but it doesn't come without some serious considerations.

IVF also carries other risks and special issues. The one we probably hear about the most is the possibility of having a pregnancy that results in multiple births. This happens because more than one embryo is usually implanted in order to increase the probability that at least one of them will take. We have all heard of women who end up carrying several babies; there is then a greater likelihood that there will be a premature delivery and one or more of the babies will suffer from low birth weight and other potential medical problems. It's no secret that IVF children frequently have a higher percentage of medical issues, including a much higher incidence of cerebral palsy.

Mothers are typically given the choice of reducing the number of viable transplanted embryos, which would most likely improve the health of IVF children, but this decision involves grave ethical considerations. Which child lives and which does not? IVF is also very expensive, and some insurance plans fail to provide coverage for this kind of procedure. If you are over forty, there is also less likelihood of the procedure being immediately successful, and you may need to do it several times, at additional cost. Mothers who conceive via IVF typically require more hospital care during pregnancy as well as a higher rate of cesarean births. I know there are single women who are strong and determined enough to go through this without the support of a partner. But I wasn't sure whether I was one of them.

If I were to make the commitment to have a child, I knew that as a single older mother, I would be facing other financial, psychological, and social challenges.

Financial: I had to be prepared to provide financially for myself and my child. Money may not make a good parent, but love alone doesn't pay the bills. Raising a child and putting that child through college is a daunting task. I knew that many single mothers struggled to meet expenses; they live beneath the poverty level. Consequently, so do their children.

Psychological: Playing the role of both mother and father puts more pressure on the single parent of both sexes. I remembered the essential role my father played when I was growing up. Would I be able to do this alone?

Social: Children of single mothers still require a full range of influences to complete their lives. I was fortunate, because I had a loving family living nearby. Nonetheless, I realized that I would have to work extra hard to make sure a child would have a full family life. I couldn't just allow the TV set or video games to take up the slack.

I did visit my priest to get his take on the ethical and moral dilemmas I might face as single-by-choice mom. And I started to go through the process of meeting with different doctors and discussing the IVF and sperm donor procedures. I went so far as going for my blood work, and I made many inquiries with regard to adoption.

At times I took my unwritten story to the next level by playing it out in my mind. Suppose my IVF succeeded. Then what? If I were over forty and without a husband, how popular would I be while dating in maternity clothes? With dating pushed aside, how would I meet a prospective partner? And while we're on the subject, how many guys would want to get serious with a single mother who chose that fate, especially through IVF? I realized that some men feel totally inadequate when faced with this reality: oh my God, she really doesn't need a guy!

I've talked to women who told me that they honestly believed that men prefer a woman who has her own child so she won't pressure them to have babies. They also think that a ready-made family can work for some guys. However, most of the men I've talked to about this tend to disagree. If a man is divorced and already has children, another child could add more complications and expense, particularly if the child doesn't have a known father. Some men end up feeling competitive; they want a lot of attention from their romantic partners, and they don't always want to share it with a child.

I recently spoke to several women who decided that having a child was the right choice and opted for IVF. These women were all fortunate, because they had support systems. Two of them ended up with beautiful twin babies, and they are thrilled that they made the choice they did.

In my own case, each time I got close to taking a definitive step toward being a single mother, I was stopped by the realization that it didn't feel like it was the right choice for me. I still envisioned having a child with a man who was also my husband. The bottom line is that the decision to become a single parent is deeply personal, and none of us should be judged unkindly, no matter what choice we make.

By the end of the summer, I found myself reluctantly back in the dating world. I continued to feel a little sad and discouraged, but I still hoped to find my Mr. Right. My friends kept encouraging me to go out and "get back in the water." Almost as soon as I stuck my toes in, I saw that the dating scene continued to be every bit as fraught with stress and challenges as I remembered.

On my second or third attempt to go out in the hopes of meeting the right someone, I did meet an attractive man in the right age group. I was standing with a friend at the bar of a local restaurant—I think it was on a Wednesday night—and an attractive guy came up to me and started to talk. Our conversation flowed as though we had known each other for years. At the end of the night, he asked me to dinner the following Monday. I went, and we had a great time. He asked me out again on another weeknight. We had a blast. After about three weeks of this, I confronted him and asked, "Why do we never go out on Friday or Saturday night? Are you married? Are you in a serious relationship?"

"I've had several previously planned engagements on the weekends," he said.

I knew in my gut that he was lying, and I was proved right when I never heard from him again.

When I was a child, every little girl had a box of panties with a different day of the week embroidered on each one. Something about this guy's approach to dating reminded me of that box of panties. Thinking about that made me laugh. I guess once again I was back in the dating world. I was laughing, which was a good thing, and I had yet another story to share with my friends.

Tonia's Tips:
Learn from My Experience
Open Up Your World

When I was in my twenties, I had very specific plans for my future: I was positive I was going to be married, and I was positive I was going to have children. My biggest question was *when* and *how many*. Then, as the years passed, I was forced to look at reality: I wasn't getting married and starting a family, and neither were many of my friends. I tried to stay positive, but I could feel my options shrinking and the world around me closing and becoming tighter. What now?

Single women need to realize that the world has changed and that they have a great many options. If you want the experience of being around children and having the sense of family that you assumed you would have, it is possible to become a foster parent. If you decide you want to become a single parent and go it alone, there are many options to help you do just that.

But perhaps you can have the best of both worlds: have gratifying relationships with children without being overwhelmed by the unrelenting grind of day-to-day child care, which includes three meals a day, tons of laundry, school lunches, and unremitting fatigue.

I enjoy the blessing of being a part of a close-knit family. We are always there for each other, and knowing this is very reassuring. I have a sister and a brother who have children.

My sister, Jolene, has two wonderful children—my niece, Alexa, and my nephew, James. My brother, Michael, has one son—my nephew Joseph. For me, my niece and nephews are the closest thing to having children of my own. Connecting with them and watching them grow and being able to spoil them is a wonderful thing.

When my brother got divorced and moved into my house for a couple of years, my nephew was with us quite a bit. I loved having him in the house. It was my chance to cuddle with him and read him bedtime stories. I would make him breakfast, play with him, bathe him, buy him rubber duckies, and, of course, try to help him see the difference between right and wrong. Having my niece and nephews in my life has allowed me to see what it would be like to have children of my own.

I realize that not everybody has siblings with children, but you may have cousins or friends who would be thrilled to have you play a role in their children's lives. They would probably be very happy if you offered to babysit or take the children to the park or the zoo.

Many hospitals also need volunteers to cuddle babies. This could give you a better idea of what it actually means to parent.

Another thing to keep in mind is that single women have a tendency to hang out mostly with other single women. Sometimes they totally avoid being with couples, and they absolutely don't take advantage of opportunities to relate to other people's children. We all know what it is like when a friend gets married and becomes part of that other world of married couples. It can suddenly seem as though you and the newly married friend are in different worlds. Make sure this doesn't happen with your friendships. Opening up your world to relationships with married friends can help you expand your horizons and help you figure out whether you really want marriage and/or children. Don't forget, your married friends might also have some single male friends or relatives.

12

Single at Forty—Whose Fault Is It, Anyway?

Not that long ago, if a woman admitted that she was over forty and single, she typically had to fight back a sense of embarrassment. She knew that many people automatically looked at a single woman of a certain age—no matter how attractive, accomplished, or successful—and thought, *I wonder what's wrong with her?* These days, of course, it can be quite different; many married women now look at their single friends enviously and think, "She's having more fun than I am!"

Currently, here in the United States, for the very first time, there are more single women over the age of thirty than there are those who are married. This is a huge societal shift. Single women are now the majority. What happened? What changed? And why? As more and more women make the choice to become single parents, we can't help but wonder how this is redefining the concept of the family unit.

Nonetheless, even though they may be living independent and satisfying lives, many of these single women still believe that their lives would be enriched by a loving marital partner. Individually, they are still asking the same question: "Why am I still single? Whose fault is it, anyway?"

Here are some of the reasons why I think there are so many more single women today, in the twenty-first century, than there were fifty years ago.

Societal Changes since Grandma's Day

Let's start by talking about the Women's Liberation Movement. Women in my generation and younger are different from our grandmothers. We grew up believing that we could have it all. We could have satisfying jobs, we could have happy marriages with loving partners, we could have children, we could have equal pay for equal work. This is a direct result of what the women's movement encouraged us to believe was in the realm of genuine possibility.

Of course, we don't want to go back to a time when women couldn't vote or were relegated to a subservient role. However, there are certainly moments when it appears that the women's movement didn't give women everything they desired. If you've ever been out on a date with a man who is sitting at a table across from you laboriously trying to figure out which of you owes an additional $1.57, you know what I'm talking about. We wanted it all, and now too often, we end up doing it all, while also paying for it.

The modern women's movement is identified with the turbulent 1960s and 1970s. During these years, the civil rights struggle and opposition to the Vietnam War all contributed to the discontent of a nation. In 1963, amid the backdrop of this growing public anger, Betty Friedan dropped another bomb when her book *The Feminine Mystique* was published. For years, Friedan had worked diligently from her suburban home to compile material for her book, which primarily addressed the issues of privileged, educated women who evolved into bored housewives. Friedan was considered the mother of the modern feminist movement, and her book debunked romantic views of home, family, and domestic bliss. Her ideology appealed to millions of women who identified with her message.

Those women who felt oppressed now had a voice. Their perceived lack of equality merged into a single cause, and Friedan reflected a common denominator among vast groups of women. Historically, big business, the government, and the prevailing society had automatically transferred status and power to men. Friedan set out to change all that. But what did she actually succeed in doing?

More than half a century after the modern women's movement laid down roots, gender roles have radically changed, but whether they have improved or not is a question that we all sometimes ask. The evolution of the women's movement and modern feminism has gotten mixed reviews from different age groups, gender groups, and political groups. So who got it right? Some believe that the movement has lost steam, while others strongly believe it didn't plow deep enough.

The women's movement fought for gender equality under the law and sought more protection for women and children subjected to abuse. It pressured lawmakers to make changes regarding domestic-violence issues and to provide family leave for working parents. In this way, the movement embraced noble ideals and choices for women.

Unfortunately, however, the number of single mothers living below the poverty line has grown steadily, while men on average still earn more doing the same jobs as their female counterparts. Still, the gap has narrowed. So the questions must be asked: Who has achieved freedom from the shackles of domestic servitude? Is it the mother who returns to the workplace but continues to carry much, if not most, of the responsibility for taking care of home and children, or her male partner, who may assume less responsibility than ever? Let's consider all the children who come home to an empty house. The quality of their lives has been compromised, and they had no part in shaping policy or the gender evolution. Is that equality for them?

I often wonder if my mother had it easier than mothers today do. Sure, society offered her fewer choices, but my father, as the breadwinner, provided her with a home, supported three children, and surrounded all of us with his love and security. I'm not saying that my mother had an easy job; no mother does. But being a mother was her job, and she took it very seriously. My parents were happy with the traditional arrangement: my dad happily brought home the bacon, and my mother cheerfully fried it up in the pan. They were a team, married for fifty-one years. They would have been married longer if my dad hadn't passed.

Am I an idealist, or am I romanticizing the image of my parents' marriage? Perhaps time has indeed gilded the past that I have preserved in my memories, but life seemed to guide us with a gentler hand back then. In my own experience, I have met very few men with my father's qualities, such as chivalry, loyalty, and honor.

I have always noticed loving husbands and idealized healthy relationships, such as the one my cousin Tonette and her husband, Charlie, enjoy. What a great couple. Also my friend Nicole and her husband, Anthony. I do actually know many happy couples. Why did they attract each other? Were they just lucky? Or was something else going on?

My parents grew up in a world in which most people honestly believed that no man could manage to cook, clean, care for a baby, or, for that matter, do the laundry. They were also fed messages that told them that most women wouldn't be able to genuinely succeed in the workplace, with the exception of "those career women," who were typically represented as being coldly ambitious and lacking in desirable feminine and maternal instincts. The women's movement helped to change all that, but as more and more women entered the marketplace and rightfully insisted on serious careers and living wages, they also realized that they didn't need to be dependent on men. In short, they could make their own money; they didn't have to get married.

Reliable Birth Control and the Sexual Revolution
But the women's movement wasn't the only societal change taking place during this tumultuous time. In the 1960s, "the

pill" went on the market, and for the first time, women had access to an effective form of birth control. In 1966, Masters and Johnson published *Human Sexual Response*, and the sexual revolution joined the women's movement in changing the way we looked at marriage and commitment. For the first time, both men and women came to the conclusion that they didn't need to be married in order to have sexual relationships.

When a man in my father's generation looked at a woman and thought, *I can't keep my hands off her*, the words "Let's get married" quickly began to form in his mouth. When a man today looks at a woman with the same thoughts, he rarely hesitates before saying, "Let's go to bed." Obviously, this means that there are fewer marriage proposals.

The Internet

How has the Internet helped to alter marriage statistics for women? When I was growing up, your romantic prospects were limited to the number of people you might meet during your dating years. There were the guys you grew up with, the guys you went to school with, the guys you worked with, the guys you met through fix-ups, and the guys you met by chance in places like gyms, museums, libraries, restaurants, and parties. Thanks to Internet dating, that's all changed. The choices now seem limitless. If you don't meet someone who meets all your criteria for the perfect partner today, there is always next week. All you have to do is tweak your profile or go on another dating site. Both men and women have become harder and harder to please. There are so many choices that many people honestly believe that if they keep searching long enough, they will find someone who has all of the very precise qualities they hope to find in a mate. Searching for the perfect partner has replaced settling into a comfortable marriage.

Internet dating makes some singles feel as though they are at an endless buffet. There are so many options that it is difficult to choose. You may be tempted to take small samples of everything and keep returning because you aren't getting the quality you want. Then, if you finally do find what you really like, somebody else may have gotten there first.

Societal Attitudes

I started this chapter talking about some of the ways earlier generations viewed single women. The truth is that most people tended to view single men with even more disdain. There was an almost immediate assumption that any man who hadn't married was truly strange. After all, they got to do the picking. Why would any man not want to be married? All of that has changed. It is now almost universally accepted that men can cook for themselves, clean for themselves, and do their own laundry, and the confirmed bachelor is no longer the exception.

Fifty years ago, because most people were married by the time they were thirty, singles didn't have as many friends who were enjoying similar lifestyles. They were often lonely. Today that is not true; there are so many singles that there is a genuine sense of unity and camaraderie. You don't have to watch married couples walking hand in hand and wallow in a sense of loneliness. It's not difficult to find somebody with whom to go out to a concert, movie, or dinner. Being single can be a lot of fun, and here and now, in the twenty-first century, there are definite perks and advantages attached to being independent and single.

Your Personal Decisions and Choices

Yes, societal changes explain some of the reasons why so many of us are not married, but there are other explanations, and these typically have to do with our own decisions, choices, and personal histories. Let's look at some of these reasons.

You Were Too Busy Building a Career

What were you doing when you were in your twenties, and some of the other women you knew were getting married? Perhaps you were getting a law degree, graduate degree, or medical or dental degree. Perhaps you were starting a business or working your way up a high and hard professional ladder. You were so busy working or studying that you ignored all those people who warned you that you needed to think about starting a family. You placed little emphasis or time on meeting the right person. Yes, you dated, but only those people you met through work, and often they were unappealing or already in permanent relationships with other women.

Many women have professions that are so demanding they barely have time to stop to breathe, let alone focus on finding a suitable partner. They don't have time for dating or recreation.

When Saturday rolls around, all they want to do is climb into their jammies, order up some food that comes in containers, and crawl under the covers. In fact, they may be so committed to their work that they don't even notice appropriate men who cross their paths.

You Were Much Too Picky

Sometimes when we are young, we don't fully appreciate the good guys. I have several friends who turned down fabulous men because they were flawed in superficial ways. One friend, Marianne, for example, was going out with Stuart, who was perfect for her. He was successful, intelligent, funny, and kind. Even more important, Stuart was completely in love with Marianne and wanted nothing more from life than to make her happy. Marianne also loved Stuart. So what was the problem? Believe it or not, it was a height issue: Stuart was five foot eight tall. In heels, Marianne was five foot nine. It drove her crazy. Her fantasy mate was always taller than she was; since Marianne felt as though she towered over Stuart, she didn't think she could live with this, so she rejected him, breaking his heart, and ultimately her own. Now, more than ten years later, Marianne continues to talk about Stuart; almost daily she questions her decision. Stuart, of course, quickly met and married somebody else who appreciates his many fine qualities. Marianne is still alone.

Many women also remember turning down dates with men who somehow didn't quite match up with the ideal romantic partner they imagined. Sometimes they turned down actual marriage proposals. Thinking back, you may also vaguely remember men who tried to start conversations with you—men you barely noticed at the time. Later, you ask yourself: why didn't I pay any attention to that guy? Then you remember: oh yes, he was wearing that hideous jacket. I didn't even give him a chance. What was I thinking?

I know women who readily admit that their expectations ruined their chances. They were looking for men who were gorgeous, successful, faithful, devoted, and fully committed to doing everything they could to please the women in their lives. They have reluctantly had to acknowledge that these men may not exist.

You Let the Right One Go

I've certainly had this thought about several of the men with whom I ended relationships. I wonder why I did what I did. I ask myself, *Did I let the right one go?*

My friend Sara is now forty-five, and she is still questioning why she ended the relationship with her college boyfriend. She had what seemed to be good reasons at the time. They were both graduating. He had a job offer in a different state. She didn't want to move. Besides, she wasn't quite ready to settle down. She honestly believed that there would be dozens of other guys out there whom she would like just as much, if not more. She was prepared to take her chances, so she broke up with him. Now, more than twenty years later, she still remembers the strength of their attraction and how much fun they had together.

You Lacked Confidence

Eye contact and confidence are important when you are trying to attract someone. I know that I often made the mistake of looking away when I saw an attractive guy staring at me. Was I shy? Or was I stupid? Or was it a little bit of both? Instead of making eye contact to let him know I was interested, I would do the exact opposite. I've seen many of my friends make the same mistake. Our lack of confidence perhaps interfered with meeting a potential match. By looking down or the other way, we gave off a signal that we were not interested, when in fact we were. Positive body language is key to meeting the right partner.

You Wasted Years of Your Life with the Wrong Person

You really loved the guy, and you were deeply committed to making it work out. However, the fact remains that you were on a marriage track, and he wasn't. Typically, he pursued you at the beginning, making you believe that you were destined to be together. But then he became less ardent, and you kept trying to recapture those magical feelings you shared at the beginning of your relationship. Perhaps he was also involved with other women; maybe he was even married. But when you threatened to leave him, he promised that everything would be okay. He would change his ways; he would be faithful; he would leave his wife; he would give up drinking and other addictions. You wanted to believe whatever it was he was saying, so you did. You gave him chance after chance after chance. You did it for a long time. When you finally broke up for the last time, it took you an extraordinarily long time to recover.

Many women waste years of their lives waiting for a man to change his ways. Some women follow this pattern with a series of different men, each time expecting things to be different. When they think back, they fully understand why they are over forty and single. This is particularly true for women who spent long years in a marriage that didn't work out.

Bad Timing—Bad Luck

Why do we meet the people we do when we do? Why don't we meet the ones we hope we are destined to meet? You remember the night your friend called to tell you about all the great guys at the party you decided not to attend because you had a slight case of sniffles. Is it possible that Mr. Right was one of those guys? Many women feel sorry for themselves and insist that their single status represents nothing more than bad luck or bad timing. If you have ever blamed bad luck for your single status, you are definitely not the only one doing this.

One or Both of You Had Commitment Issues

Yes, some men are terrified of commitment. The same is true of some women. If you have ever met a man who has problems committing himself to a relationship long term, you know what I'm talking about. The typical guy with commitment issues comes on like gangbusters, telling you everything you want to hear, but almost as soon as you respond in kind, he gets scared and starts backing off. Commitment problems are rampant in the twenty-first century. Singles of both sexes sometimes fear intimacy and everything that goes with it.

Others Interfered in Your Relationships

Many singles have at least one story of a relationship that went sour because of interference by others. Sometimes it's family. Some men are so devoted to their birth families that there is little room for a romantic partner. I've heard friends complain about men who appear to be overly attached to their mothers or their sisters; these women say they ended up feeling left out. In some instances, they even believed these mothers or sisters conspired to sabotage their relationships. I once had a boyfriend who bought me some genuinely special gifts. However, whenever he did this, his mother had a tendency to become jealous, so he felt obligated to buy her something of equal or comparable value. I also went out with at least one man whose mother didn't like me, no matter how hard I tried to please her. It was a terrible feeling. When the relationship became more serious, the mother sat me down to ask me how I was going to support her son and myself should his business fail. I thought this was over the top.

Friends who are jealous can also interfere and make trouble. When I was much younger, I remember meeting a man I liked, who seemed to really like me too. He asked me out, and I said yes. We made a date, then he called to cancel and never called again. I couldn't understand what happened. I asked people who knew him. It turned out that a mutual friend, who was interested in him for herself, told him that I was in a relationship with another man, which was not at all true. When I asked this "friend" about it, she acknowledged what happened. "I really like him," she told me. I guess she didn't really think it was fair that he would ask me out when he had never done the same with her. Obviously, this wasn't a real friend, and we're no longer in contact.

You Are Overly Comfortable with Your Single Life

If you reach your mid-thirties and are still single, it's possible that you are so settled in with your own life that you may not be doing everything you can to find a permanent partner. Typically, you have your life under control: you have supportive friends and family, and you even know where you will spend the holidays. You may have nephews, nieces, and godchildren whom you can play with and spoil. And, best of all, when you are tired of them, you can go home, knowing that a baby's cries will not be waking you at 2:00 a.m. You have so many good elements in your life that even though you want a loving partner, you have become content and almost complacent. In short, you don't want to work that hard to find someone who may shake your life up.

Of course, there are also those people—and I've spoken to many of them—who say that it wasn't until they achieved this state of single comfort that they finally met the right person.

You Have Children

You need to be certain that any new person is accepting and loving toward your children and has good intentions about working on building relationships with them. This is not always easy. Some people have been single for so long that they are unwilling to make the effort. Women also need to be certain that any man they bring into their family is a good role model and doesn't create additional problems.

Your Pets Have Taken Over Your Life

You adore your dog and/or your cat. Hugo and Ms. Fuzzy Face are your priorities. This means that if you meet someone, you have to be sure that this person isn't allergic to dander. They also need to like animals as much as you do. You need to be certain that this guy won't mind sharing the bed with a dog who snores or a cat who hogs the pillow.

Some relationship experts advise that singles get a dog, because it is so much easier to meet people on the street or park when you are walking a dog. This may be true, but it is also true that your pet might come between you and some of the potential partners you meet.

You Are Genuinely Ambivalent about the Idea of Marriage

We all know people who sabotage their chances of finding satisfying relationships. These men and women consistently seem to do everything possible to guarantee that no relationship will work. I think all of us can sometimes be guilty of this. Remember, all the experts and professionals remind us that marriage requires serious compromise. At some point, all singles need to be honest and come to terms with whether marriage is something they genuinely want. Ask yourself: do you really want to make the necessary adjustments and compromises in your life?

Tonia's Tips:
Learn from My Experience
Keep Moving-Survival Tips for the Single Woman

Everything in the universe moves continuously—the sun, the moon, and all the planets. If you stay motionless, you're out of sync with nature, and it's guaranteed that you will gradually fall behind. The world we live in is rapidly changing. We have all had to become accustomed to using our computers, the Internet, and our cell phones. We stay young and relevant by adapting to the changing times. It's especially important for single women to keep their minds as well as their hearts open to this changing world we inhabit. Here are some suggestions on how to do this.

Don't Feel Sorry for Yourself
Don't spend time dwelling on the past and blaming others, or circumstances, because your life didn't turn out the way you hoped and expected. This attitude will surely keep you moving in a negative, downward spiral. Stay upbeat and optimistic. I'm sure there are many good and pleasurable things about your life. Enjoy them!

Give Off Positive Signals
Whether you are at work, at the supermarket, or at a large party, smiling and saying hello to the people around you will help you make friends, both male and female. As far as

potential romance is concerned, it only takes one man to notice you. Walk and talk with confidence, conviction, and purpose. People are drawn to a positive aura and will want to learn more about you. It's unlikely that being shy will get you any attention. If you are at a party and there is a cute guy across the room, smile at him. If he doesn't come over to talk to you, it's his loss. Move on and smile at the next person you see, whether it's a man or woman. It's always good to make friends.

Tell People That You Want to Meet Somebody

In a nonchalant, no-pressure manner, let people know that you are single and looking to meet someone. Do this with your doctor, your dentist, your lawyer, your accountant, as well as your coworkers. You never know who they know. Introductions still exist.

Stay Up to Date

If you are not completely comfortable with using Facebook and the various dating sites and apps, it's time to get a move on. Personally, I am not naturally attracted to either social media or new technology, but I learned—and so can you. Ask a friend or a teenager you know for help, take a class at the library, or spend time playing with the technology until you feel comfortable using it. Some of the most common dating sites are Tinder (for the younger generation), Zoosk, Match.com, eHarmony, Plenty of Fish, JDate,

OkCupid, Our Time (for people over fifty), and Elite Singles, to name just a few.

Get Involved

After a long day or week's work, I understand the impulse that makes you want to stay home, order in some food, and binge on Netflix. I understand that you don't always want to go out and get involved in activities. But if you want to meet someone and you want to stay involved with the human race, your only option is to do something social. Some suggestions: head to the beach and get involved in a volleyball game; take a class; or go on a ski trip or a fishing trip (plenty of guys there). Remember, it's never too late to learn to play tennis or golf. Become a member at your local gym or Y. Try walking your dog at the park instead of around your block; get involved with an interesting charity, or become more active in the political party of your choice. Becoming a part of any of these activities will increase your chances of meeting someone as well as increasing your community of friends and social contacts; you will also be doing something positive for your health and well-being.

I know too many people who say they are tired and have given up. Don't be one of them. You are a winner and a good person who deserves a good life. Get motivated, set goals, get your butt off the couch, get your teeth whitened, and head out the door smiling.

Remember this, if you are single and over forty, you are a member of the largest group of singles in history. You are not alone. You have already been surviving the single world. You've mastered the hard part. Being single can be a lot of fun, so embrace and enjoy it.

13

Faith, Hope, and Love

Soon after my breakup with Vinnie, I sat down and started writing this book. I was almost forty years old, and I was single; I had been dating for my entire adult life, and I knew I wasn't alone. It seemed clear to me that my journey through the dating world was similar, if not almost identical, to that of millions of other women. My life had brought me in contact with many of these women: we had met and talked at the parties, restaurants, bars, and vacation spots that are so much part of the singles' scene. We had laughed and sometimes cried as we shared our stories. My experiences reflected those of many other women of my age, and I hoped that writing about my journey might help others negotiate the complexities of what it means to be an unmarried woman in the contemporary twenty-first century, where so many of the men we meet come to us as complete strangers. Let's face it, the Internet is both wonderful and wicked: yes, you could meet your true love, but you might also come into contact with an online Casanova, trolling dating sites and concealing an unstable temperament or a criminal record.

I knew that I wanted to be married, but no matter how old I was, I still didn't want to settle. I didn't just want a husband. I wanted a husband I loved, whose values I respected. I had been offered the opportunity of living in a mansion filled with La Dolce Vita clutter; my kids could have had a wealthy father to lavish them with every stupid gadget while I lunched at the club after a round of golf. But I knew what it was to be in a relationship where everything looked great on the outside, yet I wasn't feeling it on the inside. Without real love, none of it mattered.

I had come too far to start lying to myself now. Each time I ended a relationship or engagement, there were friends who thought I was nuts and told me as much: "What were you thinking?" "Why did you let him go?" "He was loaded and not hard to look at either." For the most part, I ignored the chorus of friends and relatives who tried to convince me that I had lost another good opportunity. What did they really know about what went wrong?

But I also knew that at forty, I had to ask myself some serious questions: Was I afraid of settling and marrying the wrong man? Or was I simply afraid of commitment itself? Would I have found fault with any man because no man (or woman for that matter) is perfect? I certainly had seen friends who had rejected good men because of small or insignificant flaws—height, weight, hair, or age. I also wondered about some of the men I had met, even casually. Is it possible that I had missed my chance with Mr. Right because I hadn't properly evaluated our potential for love? These are some of the questions that tumbled through my head as I began to write this book. But then, when I was more than three-quarters finished, unexpectedly, a special man arrived, and he changed the ending. Ah, it seems too good to be true, you must be thinking, like a chocolate chip cookie with no calories. Well, I couldn't believe it either.

Here's what happened. After many months of planning a trip to the Caribbean to visit a friend, bad weather and difficulties with rescheduling flights forced me to cancel. It was Thanksgiving weekend, and I was generally bummed out. In fact, when my phone rang, I considered not even answering it. It was my friend Lou, and he asked me to join him and some friends for dinner. I was tired, looking forward to an old movie on the TV and some of my mother's reheated turkey. There was no hesitation on my part when I said no. But Lou pushed and said he wanted me to meet his friend, who had just gotten divorced. I listened to Lou's pitch and answered with a weak "maybe." At the last possible minute, I threw on some clothes and prepared to go out. Lou's friend was named Brian; he appeared to be a good guy, but the atmosphere between us seemed lukewarm, and I had zero expectations that it would go anywhere.

A few days after our first encounter, Brian texted me. Now, I had once sworn I would never go out with a man who preferred texting to calling, but I had decided that I needed to be more flexible. After all, I had already spent too many nights alone and too much time with the wrong guy. Brian seemed shy but very gentlemanly. Hey, Lou liked him, and I had known Lou a long time. I would go for it.

Brian and I met for dinner at a Japanese restaurant, because I told him I loved sushi. After dinner we headed over to the bar and had a sake bomb. Brian pulled my barstool closer to him and then laid a kiss on me. I saw sparks. The kiss was great, and we just had a great connection. We ended up closing the place at midnight. The restaurant staff had to throw us out.

We dated for months. During that time, Brian and I had a few setbacks; for example, someone tried to break us apart. Was this person jealous? Did someone want to ruin my fairy-tale ending? Or was there something more to this? I did some basic sleuthing yet couldn't uncover any secrets surrounding Brian. My old doubts began to rent room in my head. I asked myself, What is wrong with you? There's got to be something about this guy that you're just not seeing. You remember all those times that the love bug bit you, and you ended up overlooking something monumental. Check again before you get hurt.

At first I brought both skepticism and hope into this relationship. I followed all the advice I have laid down in this book and left nothing to chance. Now I had a road map to follow, a master plan. I questioned everything about him—his past, his present, family, friends. No one would ever get the best of me again. People who have nothing to hide are not offended by scrutiny. I kept opening fictional closets, but there were no skeletons to be found. Now, don't get me wrong—there were a few bones, but nothing major. I had certainly seen my share of the kind of treachery and deceit that can flourish in the world of dating. I make no apologies for trying to protect my heart from being broken again. I wanted to be sure before making a big commitment, and there is no crime in doing your homework well.

Within the first few dates, Brian told me about his divorce and the circumstances surrounding it. He stated candidly that he wanted joint custody of his two children, Christopher and Jaclyn; he didn't want to be an absentee father. I admired his decision to actually be there for his kids and not just send out monthly checks. His honesty and commitment to his children brought me closer to him.

I truly loved him and his two children, who were just wonderful. Christopher is great and very handsome and has a fabulous sense of humor. I really appreciated that he always made me feel as though I was part of the family. Jaclyn is a very smart, beautiful and, in many ways, a typical girl. It was easy to get along with her, because soon after we met, I discovered that she loved shopping as much as I did.

True love is worth all the risks that come with trying to find it. I was very attracted to Brian. He has an inner strength and knows what he wants. He is not afraid to show his emotional side. At the same time, Brian is a man's man. He told me everything I wanted to hear. He told me he would have another child with me if that made me happy, he told me I was his soul mate, he told me his kids loved me and that he could see me being his wife and a wonderful stepmom. He told me he loved to travel as I do. He even told me he would go to Sunday mass with me. Was all of this too good to be true? I hope not, but only time will tell.

Brian turned fifty soon after we met. I wanted to show him how much I loved him and thought giving him a fiftieth-birthday surprise party would be a good way to do just that. I threw him a nice bash at a high-end catering hall with his friends and my immediate family. His children were a big help in planning and keeping it a secret. I knew that keeping this kind of secret was a big deal for kids of this age, and I really appreciated their help and cooperation. They both wanted to see their dad surprised, and he was. I love surprising people and giving; that's what make me feel good. The party was amazing, and Brian was so happy. I even invited childhood friends of his, and they flew in from out of town.

After nine months of dating, Brian proposed to me near the wishing well, against the backdrop of the Magic Kingdom in California. Just as Brian was proposing, a marching band came by, and I was convinced that Brian had hired them. He hadn't, but it was perfect timing. His two children were there to share this special moment with us. In fact, they were holding the camera and photographing the proposal and my acceptance. Brian had chosen a beautiful ring, and Jaclyn had hidden the ring in her carry-on. Having the children there made it even more meaningful.

Once the shock of the engagement wore off and reality set in, all the questions within these chapters revisited my thoughts. Did I really want to be married after being single and independent for so long? Answer: yes. Did I feel as though I was settling? No. Is our strong physical attraction and chemistry going to last? I believe so. Will I find out that he has a secret life? I'm confident he doesn't, but who knows. Let's face it, we all have some secrets. Oh, but what a relief it is to have finally found "the one." No more dating dilemmas, no more Internet dating and matchmaking. No more nights having dinner alone or with the wrong person. Life offers no guarantees, but I believe Brian and I have what it takes to make a lasting commitment.

During this time of my life, there was also some deep sadness. My wonderful dad was diagnosed with cancer, and everyone in my family was very anxious and worried. Marrying Brian meant that I would have to make a lot of changes. I would have to leave my house, which I had just, finally, finished renovating, to move into Brian's house, because his kids were still in school and their mother lived nearby. This necessitated moving my whole life into Brian's. It was especially upsetting, given my father's illness, because my house was seven minutes away from where my parents lived, and I was accustomed to being able to pop in and visit them frequently. I was also leaving my neighborhood and the life I knew. But I did it because I loved Brian and his kids, and there was no other way our relationship could work. I believe that true love is worth all the risks that come with trying to find it.

Of course, Brian and I argue on occasion, like any other couple; however, ten minutes later we seem to get over it. Well, most of the time. We're silly together and act like kids when no one's around. Brian and I have both been around the block a few times. I realize that to make a relationship work, you have to respect and value each other. I am not saying that our relationship is always easy. Of course, Brian has flaws, and so do I.

We had the most amazing wedding day. Our venue was great. The food, the décor, the people, and of course my husband! We had a Christmastime wedding, on December 15, and everything seemed perfect. My gown was a mermaid-style Badgley Mischka with Swarovski crystals. Jolene, Alexa, and Jaclyn wore cranberry gowns; my mom's gown was plum. Christopher was his dad's best man, and all the men looked handsome in their tuxes.

It was bittersweet, because I knew my dad wasn't feeling the greatest, and I could tell that my mom was worried about him, as we all were. However, my dad finally walked his baby girl down the aisle, and we had a father/daughter dance that I will never forget. Even though my dad was sick, he was such a trooper, and he never complained once. My dad was my hero and always will be! Our father/daughter dance was the last time I danced with him.

Once Brian and I married and the honeymoon period ended, the demands of day-to-day living set in, as they do for all couples. Let's face it: you don't really know someone until you've lived together for an extended period of time. My life was no longer mine. I lived my life now for my husband and my stepkids.

It seems people today are more focused on the *me* instead of the *we*. The storybook idea of a marriage and the reality of what it feels like to actually be married bear no resemblance to each other. Ask married friends for a shot at the truth, and they will quickly separate the facts and tell you to let go of the paperback, romanticized, fantasy version. Even couples who have lived together for years before marriage and thought they had it down to a science can find themselves without a formula to cure the problems that can appear after they take that final step. They may have been overly confident that the trial run gave them a virtual window into their actual marriage. Only fools never have doubts. Hard reality often cracks the paper-thin shell of know-it-all arrogance. Perhaps the faux marriage lacked dedication or the essential honesty required to go the distance. The core change that comes with marriage brings the individuals involved from *me* to *we*. That difference of one letter—the *m* to *w*—changes everything; it changes your whole life.

I believe that having a successful marriage can be almost as difficult as finding the right mate, yet I feel confident that Brian and I have a solid foundation on which to build a lasting union.

My parents' marriage lasted fifty-one years because they worked as a team and truly valued each other's contribution in the partnership. One person doing it all cannot overcome the many challenges that a relationship entails. In other words it takes two, as in "*t*ogether *w*e *o*vercome" whatever life throws in our path.

I've learned many things about myself from my long journey through the dating world and in the process of writing this book. I've learned that although I like things to be perfect, there is no such thing as perfect. I've learned that there are some things I can't control no matter how much I try. I've learned that things don't turn out the way you plan; remember that old saying, that God laughs when you make plans. I've learned that some people are great; others are questionable. This is true whether it's the guys you are dating or your so-called friends. I've learned that although some people want to see you fail, most are rooting for your success, because they admire perseverance and honesty, and your success gives them hope. I've learned that I've made many mistakes in my life, but I've also made some good choices. Most importantly, I've learned that I truly like to help people, and I've proven that by laying my story on the line.

Everyone's dating journey is unique. All of us think our personal stories are the worst, the funniest, or the most romantic. The whole point of dating is to find your own happily-ever-after. The more you are out there, the more you learn about yourself, as well as life in general. Not everyone will wind up getting married. That's just the truth. Some of us may discover that we prefer being single. We don't have a crystal ball to see how our lives will turn out. That's part of the adventure of life. All each of us can do is to be true to ourselves and remain realistic and optimistic.

I know that good things can happen if you're patient. Never give up. I'm excited to see what married life will continue to bring. For now, I'm going to live in the moment.

Tonia's Tips:
Learn from My Experience
Maintain a Loving Heart:
Survival Tips for the Single Woman

Any woman who has been single for an extended period of time—as I was—knows how difficult it is to maintain an open and loving heart. It's easy to become tired, jaded, and just generally fed up. No one said life was easy. No one said life was fair. No one said your life was going to turn out the way you planned. But the truth is that love is a possibility at any age. It's also true that keeping an open heart is important even if you decide that romantic love is not the priority you once thought it was.

Start by trying to better understand yourself. Know what you really want, not just what you think you want or what others want for you. You have only one life to live, and this is yours. Ask yourself some key questions: Are you positive that you really want to be married? With almost every man you meet, do you worry that you might just be settling? If that's the case, have you thought about whether or not you have a fear of commitment?

I don't advocate that any woman "settle," but I also have come to understand that relationships require a great deal of compromise. We all need to be sure that we know the difference between compromise and compromising. If you are in a relationship, you are going to have to learn to compromise on the details of life. You can do this without compromising who you are or the really important things you value.

Something I've learned is that not everybody sees things the way you do, and it's a waste of time trying to convince people to change. I also know that, despite the number of times we've all heard that you can't change anyone, many of us still don't believe that this is true, and we keep trying, with the same negative results.

Here are some other questions to ask yourself:

Are you looking for the impossible? Are your standards so rigid that no one can ever meet them? Does what you are looking for even exist? Maybe it's time to do some soul-searching about your expectations for a potential mate and make a realistic list of the five most important qualities instead of a list that is two pages of single-spaced type. Make a distinction between the things you want as opposed to the things you need.

Are you focusing on type? Do all the men you want to go out with have brown hair and brown eyes? Do they all have the same kind of background? It may be time to expand your horizons and start noticing different kinds of men. You never know.

Are you looking for love in enough places? You claim you want to meet someone, but what are you doing to look for him? If you are sitting at home watching a movie and eating popcorn, don't expect the person of your dreams to come through the television. You don't know where or when love can happen. Get out there and look around!

There are plenty of good people who are searching for the same things you are. After all, don't most of us want to find love and companionship? Being realistic about the qualities you require, avoiding patterns that have not worked for you in the past, and getting involved in more things will open your world and maximize your chances of meeting the right one.

I have met many women who say they thought they were marrying their soul mates, but once they were actually married, their husband turned out not to be the person they thought he was, and they ended up divorced. I have also met women who said that when they were walking down the aisle, they wanted to run the other way, yet they have been happily married for twenty years or more. We all know that there are no guarantees in life. Everything is a gamble. Are you ready to gamble on love?

Surround yourself with honest, true people who care about you and truly want to see you happy. When it comes to making lifelong decisions, do your due diligence before you jump into anything. And don't dwell too much on negative events. My father once told me that when you are in a situation that you think is bad, before you make too big a deal of it, ask yourself if in a year from now it will affect your life. If not, let it go. In other words, don't sweat the small stuff.

Like everything else in life, being single has both negative and positive elements. I truly believe that God helps those who help themselves. It's God's timing that counts, not yours. My journey through the dating world has brought me over the peaks and down into the valleys, that's for sure.

But I got through it. The one thought I never entertained was, "Should I forget about the whole thing?" That never happened. Perhaps the one piece of advice that I can offer with all my heart is to stay positive no matter what. It often seems as though circumstances are against you, but keep your vision, and stay patient.

And, finally, always keep your heart open to love. Over two thousand years ago, Saint Paul expressed it best in his letter to the Corinthians (Cor. 13:4–8):

> *Love is patient and kind, never jealous or envious, never boastful or proud, never haughty or selfish or rude.*
> *Love does not demand its own way. It is not irritable or touchy.*
> *Love does not hold grudges and will hardly ever notice when you are wrong.*
> *Love is never glad about injustice but rejoices whenever truth wins out.*
> *Love bears all things, believes all things, always hopes all things, endures all things.*
> *Love never fails.*
> *There are three things that remain—faith, hope, and love—and the greatest of these is love.*

Acknowledgments

My book came about as a result of my personal journey and the journey of others who were trying to find love. I am grateful to my friends and those individuals who opened up and shared very personal experiences that they had stored in the secret vaults of their hearts. Having been disappointed in love, I know personally that this was difficult but vital to the integrity and honesty of my manuscript. Surveys and statistics are important, but people make it real and authenticate the experience for the reader. I'm particularly grateful to my friends Lorraine, Susan, Madeline, Steven, Laurie, and Nicole. They have all been with me through some of my most difficult times, and I will always appreciate their support. And, of course, I could never have written this book without my ex-boyfriends, whom I forgive. I hope they forgive me.

Several people inspired and contributed to my writing in this book: Rosanne Pellicane, writer and author of *She Came from Heaven*, and Julia Sokol Coopersmith—I couldn't have written this without these amazing, talented women. I also want to thank Stephanie Susnjara, Stephanie Navatto, Sue Perrault, and Chris Ziminski for all their help.

My mother and father always encouraged me to reach beyond the predictable; they provided me with a very fine education so I could walk through life with confidence. The signature mistakes that I have printed between the covers of this book were all mine. I own every one.

I will always be grateful for all my parents taught me. I know how difficult it has been for my mom since my dad's passing, yet she has continued to be my strongest support system. Thank you, Mom, for everything. To my two siblings, Jolene and Michael, and my niece, Alexa, and nephews, James and Joseph: I am grateful for all your love and understanding over the years. My close family ties have sustained me through some rough times, and my family has cheered with me during the best of them.

I thank my husband, Brian, and stepchildren, Christopher and Jaclyn, whom I have known the shortest period of time and yet who have become such an important and integral part of my life.

Most important, I thank God for all the trials, tribulations, and mistakes I have made in my life. All of this has made me more empathetic to others and has made me appreciate life and all its learning experiences.

God gives us hope but never perfection. Live with it, and keep the faith.

About the Author

Tonia DeCosimo writes for The Date Mix, the web magazine hosted by Zoosk.com, one of the largest dating sites in the U.S. Her bi-weekly column gives Tonia the chance to share her experiences, advice, and ideas with those who are facing their own dating challenges. Tonia, a successful entrepreneur, received her B.S. degree in Elementary Education and English from Manhattan College. Her career path, however, took her into the fields of marketing, publishing and sales consulting in which she has worked successfully for the past 25 years. In that time, she has built and managed several companies, including her own.

Tonia, the proud stepmom of two teenagers, resides on Long Island with her husband.

We invite you to follow Tonia:

Website: www.toniadecosimo.com

Made in the USA
Middletown, DE
19 April 2017